SHROP

FOLK
TALES

SHROPSHIRE

FOLK TALES

AMY DOUGLAS
ILLUSTRATED BY LYNN RUST

The History Press

To Chloe, these stories are for you to read and keep. I hope they
will keep you company, guide you on your journey and remind
you that though sometimes the world can be a dark place, it is
also a place of joy, wonder and magic

and

To Sal; my friend, confidante and co-conspirator, for your keen
eye and sound judgement. Your open-hearted listening has been
an inspiration

First published 2011

The History Press
The Mill, Brimscombe Port
Stroud, Gloucestershire, GL5 2QG
www.thehistorypress.co.uk

British Library Cataloguing in Publication Data.
A catalogue record for this book is available from the British Library.

ISBN 978 0 7524 5155 8

Typesetting and origination by The History Press
Printed in Great Britain

CONTENTS

ACKNOWLEDGEMENTS

There are a large number of people whose support, enthusiasm, knowledge and generosity have helped make this book possible.

The oral tradition is alive and well in Shropshire. A wealth of heritage, wisdom and folklore is held in the memories of local communities. I'd like to thank everyone who has shared snippets and titbits of stories, anecdotes and memories.

I am particularly in debt to Mike Rust, who has been a tireless proponent for storytelling in Shropshire. He was a founding member of the storytelling club 'Tales at the Edge', the storytelling festival 'Festival at the Edge', as well as the national 'Society for Storytelling'. He has collected stories throughout his life and has been exceptionally generous with his time and knowledge during the preparation of this book.

My gratitude goes to the following for their help and positive attitudes in answering my bizarre requests, tracking down obscure references, pointing me in the direction of new stories and checking historical details: Dez and Ali Quarrèll of Mythstories Museum of Myth and Legend; Shropshire Archives, in particular Sarah Davis and Liz Young; Bishops Castle Heritage Resource Centre; the Wenlock Olympian Society and the Much Wenlock Town Archives; Father Ambrose, St Milburga's Roman Catholic Church; Wenlock Priory, English Heritage.

I am indebted to Clive Fairweather, who translated a large chunk of Latin for me when I was pulling my hair out with frustration.

Thank you to Sarah Douglas and Fiona Collins for their invaluable help in letting me sound out ideas, and to Sarah for all her time spent painstakingly proofreading.

ABOUT THE AUTHOR

Amy Douglas first discovered storytelling at the age of thirteen. Shortly afterwards, she helped Mike Rust and Richard Walker to found 'Tales at the Edge', one of the first modern-day storytelling clubs in England. At sixteen she was part of the team that launched 'Festival at the Edge', the first English storytelling festival of its kind. At nineteen, she was chosen as the first West Midland Arts Storytelling Apprentice and spent a year studying storytelling with professional storytellers throughout Britain and America. During that year she first worked with Scottish traveller and storytelling legend Duncan Williamson, the beginning of a much longer apprenticeship and friendship.

After finishing her studies, Amy became a full-time professional storyteller in 1999. She has performed in Britain, Europe, the U.S. and Canada at venues including schools, libraries, arts centres, museums, pubs and clubs as well as storytelling, literature and folk festivals. She served two years on the board of directors for the National Society for Storytelling in England and Wales.

Amy now works extensively on site-specific projects, celebrating local communities; their stories and recollections and that magical connection between the land, story and the people who live there. She is

fascinated by different learning styles in children and the impact that storytelling and the use of outdoor spaces can have. She has co-edited two books of reminiscences, *Memories of Pontcysyllte* and *Evesham Voices*. In 2005, she co-edited the award winning *English Folktales*, a collection of traditional English stories retold by English storytellers.

For more details about her work and publications, please visit Amy's website: www.amydouglas.com

INTRODUCTION

Shropshire is a large rural county on the Welsh borders. It is definitely border country, traditional English patchwork fields and hedgerows giving way to wild bracken-covered hillsides as you travel west towards Wales. The atmosphere of the Shropshire hills, and their familiar presence watching over me, has fascinated me all my life, and they all have stories of how they came to be and of the people who have walked here.

This book is a selection of some of Shropshire's folk tales. They are stories that have been handed down from generation to generation, sometimes written, sometimes only by word of mouth. These are tales that have grown up out of the landscape, clustered around certain characters, or evolved to make sense of the world around us. They are stories to entertain, to give shivering thrills on dark nights, to deal with daily life and to face common fears.

I love the power stories have. Storytelling is my hobby, my passion and now my career. Stories contain maps for the emotional world around us; they throw open doors to other worlds and other times; they take us on journeys that can lead to the other side of the world, or reunite you with those you would wish to be closest to. Storytelling has always been and, I believe, always will be a vital part of human life. A world without stories would be a world without joy and magic, a confusing and frightening place, without the experience and wisdom of those who came before to guide us.

Somewhere within them all stories carry a grain a truth, that speaks to us and makes the story live within us. But these stories are not historically accurate. Stories have grown up around historical events, places and people; they can give insight into the character of those times and how they were viewed by the people. They often contain detail that has been left out of the history books. Just as frequently, the story that survives could never have happened the way it was told. I haven't found any proof of a piece of tax-free land near Astley Abbots, as claimed in the story of Collen and Sabrina. There is no evidence to support the cruelty of Squire Pigott; the estate was sold in about 1780 for reasons that had nothing to do with Madam Pigott's haunting. But once a story has caught hold of the imagination it will not let go. In *Shropshire Folklore* Charlotte Burne describes the spirit of Madam Pigott being laid twice, and concludes that she no longer troubles the neighbourhood. Yet over a century later, everyone in Newport has a story to tell of where she haunts or of a friend who has seen her.

There are always occasions where the dates don't quite add up. Stories are clothed in the details of daily life – a story may be set a thousand years ago, but the day-to-day details are those familiar to the teller, or what the teller imagines as old fashioned.

For me, these anachronisms and fanciful additions enrich the stories rather than diminish them. I love the way that stories grow with communities, becoming interwoven with their landscape, personality and daily life.

Storytelling is an intrinsic part of human nature and there are stories wherever there are people. That said, Shropshire seems to have a particularly rich vein of folklore and storytellers. Over the past couple of decades, storytelling has enjoyed a resurgence throughout the country and Shropshire has been at the forefront of the revival. There are well-established storytelling clubs flourishing in Wem, Bridgnorth, Bishops Castle and Shrewsbury. It is home to 'Festival at the Edge', an annual weekend celebration of storytelling on Wenlock Edge. Mythstories Museum of Myth and Legend, the only museum of its kind in England, is based in Wem and is also home to the Society for Storytelling's library.

Amy Douglas, 2011

MAP OF SHROPSHIRE

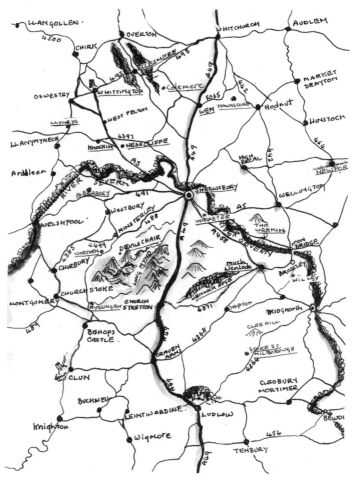

Decorative map of Shropshire, based on the 1932 OS ten-mile road map. The locations of stories are underlined.

One

In the Beginning

The Making of the Wrekin

The Wrekin is one of the great landmarks of Shropshire.
I grew up in its shadow and when I see its familiar outline,
I know I am not far from home. There are few places in
Shropshire where the Wrekin cannot be seen. It rears up in
the flat Shropshire plain: from Cressage and the south, a sharp
conical peak; from Shrewsbury and Newport, a long undulat-
ing ridge, a great sleeping body sprawled across the land.

The Wrekin is one of those places that become enwrapped
in people's lives and traditions. For many local people, walking up the Wrekin on Boxing Day or New Year's Day is an
integral part of the season's ritual. For many years, one family
climbed the hill each Christmas Day to eat their dinner on
the summit! I always meet my mother there to walk through
the bluebell glades in May. To go 'all around the Wrekin' is the
Shropshire version of going all around the houses. The toast,
'To all friends around the Wrekin', is still regularly used, particularly at New Year.

Long, long ago when the Earth was new, in the time when animals and humans talked the same language and giants roamed the land, there were two brothers, two giants.

The giants were looking for somewhere to make a home. They roamed all over the Isle of Britain until at last they came to the flat plain of Shropshire. There they decided to build their home; a great mound of earth, where they could see for miles all around them.

That's when the work began. The two brothers had a spade, just one spade between them, and they started to dig. They took it in turns, one brother using the spade, the other scrabbling with his hands. They worked hard, sweat dripping from their brows. The work was tough for both giants, but harder for the brother digging with his hands than for the brother with the spade. Hot and tired, they began to argue, fighting over whose turn it should be to use the spade.

The spadeless giant tried to grab the spade from his brother and the two wrenched it back and forth, each determined to use it. Soon the giants were hitting and kicking, biting and scratching, pulling and tugging. The spade twisted and turned between them, slicing into flesh instead of soil. The giants' angry roars rolled like thunder across Shropshire. The ground shook as they tussled.

Up in the sky, a raven was wheeling on the wind. He saw the great giants fighting below and that the giant with the spade was winning, his brother growing weak. The raven waited for its chance, then dived down. Suddenly, the giant's face was full of feathers. A terrible cry rent the air as the raven pecked out the giant's eye. Clutching his face in agony, the giant dropped the spade. One great tear rolled down his cheek and fell to the ground.

Quick as lightening, his brother grabbed the spade and hit his sibling over the head. The giant's knees buckled; he swayed from side to side and, like a tree trunk, he slowly toppled, gathering momentum until he hit the ground. The earth shuddered; the giant lay still.

His face was full of feathers

The giant's body mingled with the earth that was to be his home. Days turned to weeks, months turned to years, decades turned to centuries. The soil was blown over his body. The grass and flowers took root, and then slowly the trees spread their branches overhead. Beneath the trees came minibeasts and rodents, birds and mammals, until the woods were teeming with life, all making their home on the giant's bones.

Many people have now forgotten the giant, but if you look at the Wrekin, you can still see the shape of his body lying beneath the earth. On the steep, southern side of the Wrekin, looking towards Little Wenlock, is the Needle's Eye, a cleft in the rock left by the spade during the fight. Lower down the slope is a basin, the Raven's Bowl, formed from the giant's tear, where there is water to be found even in the driest summer.

Severn

Happy is the eye between Severn and Wye
But thrice happy he, between Severn and Clee

Long, long ago, Plynlimon, lord over hill and mountain, field and forest, called his three daughters to his side. He looked at each fondly: fair Severn, serious and thoughtful; red-headed Wye, smiling and serene, and dark-haired Rheidol, impetuous and carefree. He smiled at them all and said:

My daughters, you are grown women now and I am an old man. It is time for me to rest my bones and for you to take over the care of the land. The hour has come for me to share my land amongst you. Tomorrow, each of you must travel from here to the coast, and you will be Queen over all the land you traverse. You have the whole day, from sunrise to sunset, but if you do not reach the sea by sunset, be warned, you will lose your share.

The three sisters looked at each other with growing excitement, each beginning to make plans for her journey.

Severn went to bed early that night and was awake and ready while the stars still shone. She sat waiting in the cold before dawn, watching the east slowly lightening until the sun crested the horizon, then she was up and away like a hare. The sea lay to the south, but instead she headed towards the rising sun, intent on making the most of her day and covering as much ground as possible. Behind her she left a swallow to watch her sisters, to warn her when they woke and set out on their way.

Wye thought about her route, readied herself in her mind and slept at her usual time. She woke with a yawn and a stretch, then smiled as she remembered what the day held. Wye set off in the early morning sunshine, determined to enjoy her day and claim land that she loved. She gently made her way southwards, picking her way through vales and meadows.

As Wye woke, the swallow watching her shook out its wings and took to the skies. The messenger sped east to tell Severn that Wye had begun her journey. As the swallow swooped around Severn's head, Severn turned and headed for the coast. Strong and determined, her long strides carried her mile after mile.

Rheidol had planned to be away at first light like her sister Severn, but in her excitement she tossed and turned, sleep eluding her until almost dawn. When at last she woke, her sisters were long gone and the sun was high in the sky. In panic she leapt up and headed at breakneck speed for the sea, jumping down boulders, clambering over precipices, desperately racing to reach the coast in time.

Evening approached and all three daughters reached the shore. Severn and Wye's paths joined together and they held hands for the last few steps of their journey. As the sun sank beneath the horizon, the three girls ran from land to sea. As each stepped into the salt water, she turned into a river. Plynlimon, watching from his distant seat, saw their journeys complete, sighed and settled into the form of a mountain. So the family remains: Plynlimon watching over his three daughters, nurturing and nourishing them; Severn, Wye and Rheidol forever tracing the paths they took long ago on a summer's day.

On her journey to the sea, Severn makes her way through the heart of Shropshire, dividing the county in two. She is beautiful and wild, serene in summer with the sun sparkling on the water, frightening in spate when the churning brown waters break their banks and cause disruption and chaos, flooding houses and roads. It is true, even today, that the river claims at least one soul every year.

They say that a person who drowns another in the Severn must never again attempt to cross the river in a boat, for long arms will reach up from beneath the water, pull them from the boat and drag them down, down, down beneath the surface. Whether they cross it or not, the river will call the murderer back to the spot that heard their victim's 'drowning scream'.

The river, in all her names (Severn in English, Hafren in Welsh, Sabrina in Latin), is always feminine. She twists and turns in sensuous curves; a beautiful surface with treacherous currents beneath.

Severn has always been an integral part of the lives of the people who live close to her, and there are stories all along the banks of the river, from source to sea. In Bewdley, legends cling to Blackstone Rock: tales of a lost ring in a salmon's belly and the river rocking lost infants safe to the hermitage. Further downriver are myths of both the River God Nodens and of Sabrina, the River Goddess, riding the Severn Bore in her chariot, with dolphins and salmon attending her. In Shropshire, the Devil claims the souls of men caught fishing on a Sunday and rides up and down the river on a coracle, fishing for drowned souls. Then there is the story of a lonely fisherman who lived on the banks of the river, lulled to sleep each night by the song of her waters. He would dream of Severn's cool caresses, the sigh of her soft silken touch rippling over him, and the lilting tones of a woman's voice within the endless, mesmerising flow of water to the sea.

The fisherman's name was Collen. He had a little plot of land, close to where the river flowed, but set high enough to miss the worst of Severn's moods and seasons. Collen was a shy man, used to his own company. His parents were long gone and he had always been on the outskirts of the village, never joining the dances or season's revels. He got by, scratching a living from his patch of land and the fruits of the river.

It was September. The days were shortening and there was now a chill in the shadows and the night time. The salmon were returning from their wandering and swimming upriver. Collen climbed into his coracle, armed with his fishing line and a packet of food, and paddled upstream. It was a beautiful afternoon, a last golden echo of summer. The autumn rains had not yet arrived and the river travelled gently between her banks, slow and steady towards the sea. Collen was headed towards Cressage, to the meanders where the river slowed and formed pools of calm water on the inside of the bends, where the salmon could rest before continuing on their journey.

Collen quietly skulled around the bends, looking at the shade on the water and feeling the currents as they pulled the coracle. He found a perfect spot; shadows from overhanging trees dappled the water and the coracle needed only the lightest of touches to prevent it from drifting back into the current. Collen took his line, three hooks dangling from it, and cast it out across the water.

Though Collen had judged the day as ideal for an after-noon's fishing, luck was not with him. He cast time and again, but each time the line lay untouched, the hooks empty. The sun was sinking in the sky, afternoon turning to evening. Collen cast his line one last time; this time the line jerked. Steadily, firmly, he pulled the line in, the fish twisting and jerk-ing, fighting to be free. Collen hauled the fish into his boat and took a firm hold to take out the hook. He held the flapping fish in his hands and the warm evening light of the setting sun gleamed against her shimmering scales. Collen stared down, entranced. The fish stopped struggling and lay quietly in his arms, looking up at him. He traced the meridian line on her side, the dark colours on her sleek sides, her silvery white belly. Looking at her, a lump caught in Collen's throat. She was per-fect: supple and strong, graceful and wild. He stared down at her and she stared right back up at him. There was no denying the intelligence in those eyes.

Collen couldn't do it. He couldn't kill her, couldn't smack her head on the side of the boat. In a single sudden move-ment he heaved the fish away from him, over the side of the coracle and into the water. Collen then skulled himself over into the current, cursing his weakness and stupidity, and the wasted afternoon. He had obviously been living on his own for too long.

The magic and stillness of the afternoon was broken. Collen shivered. The day's warmth was gone and it was time to head home. In the wake of the boat, a sliver of silver turned and swam downstream. The current took the coracle swiftly on its way, but night had fallen by the time Collen reached home. He was glad of the full moon as he splashed out of the boat to haul the coracle up onto the bank out of the water.

That night, Collen woke to singing. He lay on his pallet and listened. There was no doubt about it; there was the usual song of the river, but mingled in with the water was a woman's voice. Collen pulled himself from his bed, opened the door and stepped out into the night. The moon was high in the

sky now, but still lighting up the night, reflecting bright from
the river. There was a woman swimming in the water. Her
skin gleamed white in the moonlight, and he realised she was
naked. She swam towards the bank and climbed out, water
streaming from her skin. The night was still. Collen looked at
the maiden, her long hair caressing her shoulders and tumbling to her waist. She smiled at him, holding out her hands,
and in the moonlit dreamworld Collen took her hands and
the two lay on the bank together, no words spoken or needed.

In the morning, Collen woke in his own bed, hair tousled
and memory tangled in dream. He shook his head to clear his
senses and saw the woman lying next to him, her skin pale as
moonlight. Only now did he see the cut in her cheek, where
her delicate flesh had been snagged by a barb. She opened her
eyes, saw him looking down at her and smiled. Her name was
Sabrina and she never left.

Collen and Sabrina lived in contentment on the banks of the
Severn, and they began to fill their home with children. People
talked, as people always do, but in time the talk moved on.

One day, King Merewald and his family rode out visiting,
stopping by the river to walk and picnic. They were talking
and walking; the King, Queen and their young family. The
eldest princess, Milburga, was only seven or eight years old,
the youngest still a babe in arms. As they talked, the Queen
absentmindedly played with a ring on her finger. Whether it
was a swan skidding to land on the water, making her jump, or
she stumbled over a tuft of grass, no one was sure, but something distracted her. The ring tumbled through her fingers,
bounced down the bank and into the current. The Queen
was devastated and the King called immediately for someone
to retrieve the ring. A couple of his men lowered themselves
down from the bank and waded around in the water looking
for the glint of the ring, but they only made matters worse,
churning the sediment up into the water. Another of their
attendants rode off for aid and a little while later, a couple
of coracles approached to help the search. Soon, people were

Pole in the water

coming from all directions to see the excitement and catch a glimpse of the King and Queen.

Almost unnoticed, a young woman slid into the river, but Princess Milburga was watching. She saw the smooth grace as the woman dived, and then a flash of silver beneath the surface of the river. She watched wide-eyed; there was no longer a woman searching the water, but a salmon. A little while later the young woman emerged, her golden hair wet, sleek and shining down her back, gold glinting in her palm. She quietly made her way to the Queen, took her hand and wrapped her fingers around the ring. She would have slipped discreetly away, but the Queen held onto the woman's hand and bid her stay. The search was ended and the King was so delighted he declared that, as long as the woman and her family stayed on their piece of land, they would never have to pay taxes again.

To this day, it is said that there is a piece of land near Astley Abbotts that has never been sold and remains in Collen and Sabrina's family still. Over a millennium later, you will still find people near that stretch of the river with strawberry blond hair that shimmers like scales; they have a certain tilt to the chin and a birthmark like a little scar from their top lip to their cheek.

TWO

SAINTS AND SINNERS

SAINT MILBURGA

It was a time of change. The old ways that everyone had taken for granted were being challenged. Word of a new God, a new faith, a new way of life, was sweeping across the land.

Milburga embodied all the hopes and dreams of the new times. She was radiant with youth, delighting in the world around her and all its daily miracles: the changing seasons, a flower opening, a bird taking flight. Whenever she passed by, it seemed that the birds would sing a little sweeter, the flowers lift their heads and the grass grow greener in her wake.

Milburga was the eldest daughter of Merewald and granddaughter to Penda himself, King of Mercia. During his rule, through the seventh century, Mercia had grown in strength, size and reputation. Penda had ruled in the old ways, holding fast to the old beliefs and resisting the new faith that was catching like fire across the land. But now King Penda was dead, the great oak had fallen and the wind was changing. His three sons, Wulfhere, Ethelred and Merewald, turned their backs on the old beliefs and were baptised into Christianity. The sons ruled Mercia between them as Christian Kings, and Merewald held Maegonsaeton – the Forest of Dean, Herefordshire and South Shropshire. Merewald settled near the place where Much Wenlock is now. He raised his family in the new faith and let it guide him as he ruled.

Milburga grew up with a sense of wonder at the world around her. Her spirit was nurtured by her parents' belief and love, and all Milburga ever wanted to do was to devote her life to God. In all the beauty around her she felt his love and wanted to celebrate it with the world.

However, Milburga was a princess of wealth and high standing, and she was fast growing into a beautiful young woman. The lilt in her step and her shining eye caught attention. Suitors came courting and her lack of interest only succeeded in making her more tantalising to them.

One neighbouring prince determined to marry her, despite her father's refusals and Milburga's resistance. One day, Milburga was out riding when she heard the baying of the hounds. She slowed and turned to see the prince and his retinue out hunting. The prince felt her eyes upon him and looked up to see Milburga seated on her white mare. The corners of his mouth curled up. He called back his dogs and set them hunting a different prey.

For a moment, Milburga stared, perplexed, then her mare reared and turned, bolting away from the hounds speeding towards them. Milburga urged her on, but soon the mare's flanks were heaving and the hounds were gaining, snapping at their heels. Ahead of them was the River Corve. With a desperate effort, Milburga's mare gathered herself and leapt for the other side. As her hooves landed on the far bank, the water swelled up behind her, roiling against the banks, an uncrossable torrent.

The prince cursed. But his blood was up and he would not give in so easily. He found a ford upriver and continued his pursuit over the Edge and beyond.

Milburga's flight took her through forest and field, over the rise of the Edge, along the Corvedale, until at last she found herself in the Clee Hills. Exhausted, she fell fainting from her horse. Her head struck stone and a crimson halo bloomed on the ground beneath her. Some peasants were sowing barley in the field beside the road. They saw her slide from her horse and came running to help. They cradled her head and called for water to cleanse the wound, but there was none to be had. Milburga's eyes fluttered open and weakly she gestured to her horse. The mare struck her hoof on the rock and at once a spring of water gushed out. As the men bathed Milburga's head, the edges of the wound closed together and the colour came back into her cheeks. Ignoring the men's protestations, she slowly rose to her feet and looked about her. For a moment all weakness fell away, leaving her stood tall, a halo of light surrounding her.

She looked at the spring and said, 'Holy water, henceforth and forever flow freely.' She turned to the new-sown barley field, 'Grow!' she commanded.

The light faded and she slumped a little, the exhaustion once again written on her face. Though the field hands begged her to stay, she refused and instead remounted her horse.

The farm men watched her go. When they turned back to the field, there was already a green haze over the bare earth. As the day went on, the barley grew taller and stronger, at last turning from green to gold, and, that very same evening, the barley was ready to harvest. The men were sharpening their sickles when they heard the baying of the hounds and the clattering of the hooves.

'Where is she? Have you seen the lady in white? When did she pass this way?'

The peasants looked up at the prince and his travel-stained band. Not one harvester removed the cap from his head.

'Yes, we saw her. But it was a long time ago now. She came as we were sowing this barley that we are just now harvesting.'

At last the prince, in bafflement, gave up his chase and Milburga was able to make her way home safely. She left

behind the spring and the bloodstained stone. The village
became known as Stoke St Milborough as the story spread,
and pilgrims came to the spring for its healing water.

Milburga returned home and the stories came following
after her. They confirmed everything that her parents had
already begun to believe about their daughter. Milburga left
for Chelles, near Paris, to be instructed and inducted into
the Church, while at home Merewald built a monastery – a
double monastery, with quarters for both nuns and monks,
and two churches, so that all would be welcome to worship.

When Milburga finished her training, she came back to
Wenlock Abbey and became Abbess; she was still only eighteen. Slowly a town grew up around the abbey, the beginnings
of Much Wenlock. Throughout her time as Abbess, Milburga
was known as a woman of power and mercy. She watched over
the town and its environs, and everyone, of high or low degree,
knew that if they needed help, her door was open.

One year there had been a hard winter, even more so
than usual. Although the days were lengthening, it didn't feel
as though spring was on its way. The farmers had ploughed
the fields, cracking the earth that was like iron with the frost.
But when they sowed the seed, clouds of wild geese, hungry
from the winter, came and settled over the fields, devouring
the grain. All the fields had scarecrows, the boys were sent
out with bird-scarers, but the geese took no notice. The crops
needed to be sown, but it seemed there was no way to protect
them. At last, in desperation, a delegation of farmers went to
the abbey to ask for help. Milburga listened and smiled.

'Of course I will help. If you cannot do your work, then
we all suffer,' she said. The farmers followed Milburga out
of the abbey and into the fields. They watched as she stood
in the centre of a field, stretched out her arms and called
the geese down to speak with her. The sky darkened. Waves
of geese came flocking through the air, settling on the bare
earth, so that Milburga stood in the centre of a sea of birds.
The farmers saw her talking, nodding and smiling with the

geese. At last, she raised her arms up into the air and the geese followed, filling the air with feathers once again. From that moment until her death, not one goose landed on any field under Milburga's protection.

Milburga watched over the abbey and the new town growing around it. She made it her business to know all the people under the abbey's care. She walked in harmony with the seasons and there was a contentment that blanketed the land while Milburga was Abbess. She loved to have soil under her fingernails and spent as much time as she could in the abbey gardens. She planted and tended her flowers and herbs so that the gardens were beautiful all year round. The scent on a summer breeze would drift for miles around and make people stop and smile. She taught her novitiates how to make poultices, ointments and medicines from the plants she grew, but it was her listening ear and gentle, firm manner that would ease the pain in her congregation's hearts and mend rifts between neighbours.

Milburga ruled the abbey for more than thirty years and, throughout her life, she built up the assets of the monastery, trying to ensure that her charges would be financially secure when she could no longer look after them. When she felt her end drawing near she made a will, setting down all the assets and everything due to the monastery.

At last her time came. She gathered her followers around her bed, blessed them one by one, sighed, and closed her eyes. A beautiful smile crept over her face.

Times change and nothing remains constant. There was unrest in the borders. The Welsh came raiding from the West, while from the East came the Danes. Many monasteries were destroyed, attacked for their wealth and their faith. Wenlock Abbey survived, but it suffered. The nunnery closed, and the abbey became a college of canons. Many of the buildings fell into disuse and dilapidation and, over time, even the place of Milburga's grave was lost.

But the wheel turned again. With the arrival of William the Conqueror, the fortunes of the Catholic Church improved. Around 1080, monks from La Charité-sur-Loire arrived in Wenlock, took over the monastery and began to restore and add to it. When they first came, the new Minster church had recently been built by Leofric, for public worship, but much of the monastery was in disrepair. The monks had Priory Church for their prayers and services, but the old Holy Trinity Church was falling apart. The rain came in through the roof, the inside was damp and anything perishable was rotting away. The monks worked hard to restore the buildings. They also worked hard to restore the local faith, belief and trust in the Lord and, more to the point, the monks as his servants.

One day, Raymond, a servant working on the restoration of Holy Trinity, found a mouldering box; inside it were various documents written in English, which the monks could not decipher. For a while they were put to one side and forgotten, but as they settled and built more links with the community around them, they at last found a translator. The manuscripts were written by a priest called Alstan, who testified that Milburga was buried near the altar. This caused a certain level of excitement, but there was no clue as to exactly where she might be buried. The altar was now derelict through neglect and pagan violence. They sent word to the Archbishop of Canterbury, and he gave permission for the monks to dig within the church in order to prove, or disprove, the truth of the document. In the end the monks did not need to dig.

It was the feast of St John the Baptist and the monks were performing the night office in the Priory Church. Two boys had slipped into the Church of the Holy Trinity and were playing amongst the tools and ongoing work. Suddenly, the ground beneath them gave way and they tumbled into a pit. They lay there, stunned, surrounded by an overwhelming, beautiful smell, the scent of a myriad herbs and flowers in full bloom, as though they had fallen into a garden.

The boys were not alone in the church. There were several other people present, including Raymond, who, once he had helped haul the boys out of the pit and confirmed they were unhurt, went running to the Priory Church. The monks were singing matins as Raymond came into the church. They saw him whispering in the ear of Richard, their Prior, and pulling at his habit; Raymond was bright-eyed, impatience simmering in every line of his body. In a moment, both Richard and

Raymond were running out of the church to the wide-eyed
wonder of the rest of the congregation.

It was too dark to see or do anything that night, but a
tantalising remnant of the scent lingered – enough to give
Richard hope that they had at last found St Milburga's
resting place. The next morning, he announced the happen-
ings of the night to the monks and they began to dig in
the pit. They found rust-eaten iron bands and, with them,
beautiful, luminous bones. Among the bones were scraps of
letters, lovingly written by the saint's followers. They told
of Milburga's divine nature: how her veil once slipped from
her head and instead of falling to the ground, floated in the
air until replaced; how she had made a blind man see and
brought a corpse back to life. The bones were gently washed
and placed in a temporary shrine.

At last the church was restored. Wenlock held a great
celebration and rededication. The crowning glory of the celebration was the ceremonial enshrining of Milburga's bones.

Not long after the discovery of Milburga's remains, Bishop
Odo, the Cardinal Bishop of Ostia, arrived at Wenlock. Of
course, the priory was buzzing with news of the finding of
Milburga's bones. Odo was delighted to be at the priory at
such an exciting time, and documented the restoration and the
effects of the saint's remains. A goodwife at Peteley had been
suffering for some time from a mysterious disease. No one
could tell the cause or the cure. With all the talk and wonder
around Milburga's remains, Odo wondered if perhaps they
might finally be able to help. He gave her some of the water
that had been used to wash Milburga's bones. Immediately
she clutched her stomach, began retching and vomited up a
worm. It had two horns on its head, six legs and two horns
on its tail. Once recovered from the shock, the woman made
a full recovery.

Word spread of this miracle and pilgrims came flocking to
the shrine to be healed. Odo stayed on at the monastery to
write Milburga's story and to observe, validate and record the

miracles. Many of the pilgrims were cured, particularly those suffering from blindness or leprosy.

Over the years, Wenlock Priory continued to be a place of wonder and healing. Three centuries later, when the monastery buildings were once again undergoing repairs, several monks fell during the works and should have been maimed or killed, but were brought back to life and health by being shown an image of the saint.

In the 1520s, two children accidentally drowned while playing. Their distraught parents brought them to Milburga's shrine and the children coughed back into life.

But the landscape of politics and religion was changing. The monasteries were under attack again, and revering saints and relics was no longer acceptable. In 1547, the last year of Henry VIII's rule, there was a public bonfire in the market place. The bones of St Milburga, together with sacred images from neighbouring churches, blazed by the entrance to the church gate.

But still she is remembered. Her name is written in the landscape she loved. People still worship at holy places dedicated to her in Church Stretton, Beckbury and Stoke St Milborough. Visitors still travel to see her abbey, now Wenlock Priory, in the footsteps of the pilgrims before them. Her story is still told.

WILD WILL OF WENLOCK

There was a new Prior at Wenlock Priory, John de Tycford, and everyone seemed to breathe a sigh of relief. John de Tycford was a breath of fresh air. After years of raising taxes to pay for endless building work under Prior Humbert, the priory was ready for a change. John de Tycford was young, for a Prior, and charming. He seemed determined to work for the good of the priory and put right all the wrongs. Shortly after his arrival, a visitation of Priors came to inspect his progress.

Although they found the priory deeply in debt, they left well-pleased by the idealistic young Prior. They were convinced that John was dedicated to the wellbeing of the priory and putting the finances back in order.

John de Tycford was equally well-pleased with the visitation. But Tycford was not what he seemed. He was ambitious, manipulative and hungry for power. His eye was on the Bishopric of Rochester. Now the building work had finished, Wenlock was one of the richest priories in the country; the heavy debts were fabricated purely to line John de Tycford's pockets. Tycford was lavish in his granting of rights of St Milburga's land and assets, securing friends and favours in high places, paving his way for promotion. For a long time his charming smile and sincere manner fooled everyone.

Though on the surface all seemed well, cracks slowly began to appear in John de Tycford's veneer. Most people found them easy to ignore; it was easy to accept the Prior's reassurances. But one monk, William of Broseley, began to feel uncomfortable. William was not an ambitious man. He had no desire for leadership or power; he simply wanted to spend his days in quiet prayer and honest work. But it seemed the Lord had another destiny in mind for William. At first it was nothing he could put his finger on, just a growing unease in the pit of his stomach. But things didn't add up – literally. Some of the transactions agreed by the Prior were unfathomable, and William felt compelled to look through the Prior's dealings and the priory's accounts. At last he confronted the Prior. John de Tycford listened to all he had to say. He smiled at him and talked about the responsibilities and intricacies of leadership, how he appreciated William's concern and how the Church needed honest, conscientious souls like William. He told William there was no need to worry, put his arm around Will's shoulder and escorted him from his chambers. A few days later, William discovered he was to be transferred to Northampton.

William sat on Wenlock Edge, wrestling with his conscience. He looked out across Shropshire and contemplated

WILL sat on wenlock edge THINKING

his future. Now he knew for sure that John de Tycford was up to no good, William could not ignore the truth of it. It seemed God had chosen him as his instrument to combat the Prior of Wenlock. William was not sure he wanted to be so favoured by the Lord. He never went to Northampton, but hid on Wenlock Edge, as a renegade, waiting for his opportunity.

William had never dreamed he would end up as a criminal. His intention was to expose the Prior and his wrongs, then return to a peaceful life. When he realised that Robert de Trilleck, the Sheriff of Salop, was hunting him, he thought his opportunity had come: here was his chance to reveal to the Sheriff the corruption within the priory. Robert could prove that the Prior was a crook on a far greater scale than William could ever be, and so William gave himself up at Wenlock. The Sheriff was unsurprised by Will's accusations. With dawning comprehension, Will realised that the Sheriff already knew about the Prior and didn't care. The Sheriff laughed when he saw Will's sudden understanding and frustration, and then locked him in a prison cell in Bridgnorth.

No one was more surprised than Will when the door opened. There stood the Sheriff and a monk from the priory. The Sheriff's lips curled back in a thin smile. 'Nice to meet you, Will. You know where we are, any time you want to come and stay again,' he said, as the monk took Will's arm and guided him out.

'How did you get me out?' asked Will. 'More importantly, why did you get me out? I am not going to Northampton.' Will tried to pull his arm free from the monk's grip.

'Don't worry, Will. I want to join you. I know why you left, I know about the Prior and the Sheriff is as bad or worse. He was happy enough to set you free, once I made it worth his while.'

'You bribed the Sheriff?!'

'Easily. Something must be done, Will, and I think God has chosen you.' The monk held out his hand. Will hesitated for a moment, then clasped it with a grin.

That was how it started. William began a campaign to reclaim the money the Prior used for bribes and favours, and give it back to the people worst off and suffering most under the Prior's taxes and the Sheriff's greed. At first it was just a few monks from the priory that stood up to John de Tycford, but soon local men joined them, bringing a stream of accusations against the Sheriff, his bailiffs and 'Keepers of the Peace'.

It was widely acknowledged that Robert de Trilleck treated
the laws of the King with contempt, unless he could use them
to his financial advantage. Secluded in the priory, William had
not realised how hard life was for the common workers. Time
and again they heard tales of the Sheriff and his underlings
taking bribes to remove names from court summons; taking
monies due to the King and pocketing them, and of innocent
families thrown into prison while their homes were plun-
dered and pillaged. Over and over they heard cases such as
Lovekin's, a fisherman of Caldbrook. A couple of 'Keepers of
the Peace' arrested him for no reason and, without a warrant,
seized a crate of fish and two silver shillings, before taking him
to prison, where the Sheriff held him until Lovekin paid two
marks for his freedom.

William and his band took up arms. No longer was he
William of Broseley, the monk; instead he was Wild Will of
Wenlock. He and his band became highwaymen along
Wenlock Edge. They let normal drovers, pilgrims and merchants pass freely, but travellers on priory business were
stopped, and money from, or for, the Prior's coffers was con-
fiscated and redistributed to local people. When any of Robert
de Trilleck's underlings were caught passing that way, they
were dressed to show their crimes and tied to a tree; a message
was then sent to Trilleck. One man's plunder had included
linens, cloaks and chemises; he was left in nothing but a che-
mise. When one of Lovekin's intimidators was caught, he was
left standing in a crate of rotten fish. On one occasion, the
Sheriff came to release one of his men, to find he had been
smeared with bacon fat, and strips of bacon left between
his back and the tree. The man was wriggling and writhing,
unable to escape or brush away the ants that covered his body.

Outside of Shropshire John de Tycford and Robert de
Trilleck were well respected. Of course, the news that came
out of Shropshire was mainly filtered through their minions.
While Wild Will tried to expose the Sheriff and Prior for the
crooks they were, rumours sped around England of a fierce

band of armed monks seeking to ambush and kill the holy Prior of Wenlock.

The King issued a government order to all Sheriffs and bailiffs to arrest the vagabond monks. Trilleck had cause to regret releasing Will so cheaply. He regularly organised sweeps through the forest to try and flush out the band, but as soon as the Sheriff's men appeared, Will and his followers seemed to vanish like mist. For ten years Wild Will and his band lived in the woods on Wenlock Edge, harrying the Prior and Sheriff, giving hope to the common people, but eventually, Will's luck ran out. The Sheriff finally captured Will and, this time, would not accept payment for his release. Guarded by an armed escort to prevent his rescue, he was taken to Oswaldslow and executed on 2 August 1283.

But Will had set wheels in motion. Justice was served and eventually John de Tycford and Robert de Trilleck were thwarted. The Sheriff's fatal mistake was taking monies due to the King. The King ordered an enquiry which uncovered Robert de Trilleck's widespread corruption, and he was punished accordingly. John de Tycford received another visitation from the Cluniac Order. This time they discovered his deception and misuse of funds. He was removed from office at Wenlock in 1284 and never did receive a Bishopric, though his last act as Prior was to sell, in advance, the wool crops for the next seven years and take the money with him.

HUMPHREY KYNASTON

Humphrey Kynaston had a good start in life. He was son of Roger Kynaston, Castle Keeper of Myddle Castle and Knockin. When his father died he inherited a large estate and a sizeable fortune. He did not inherit his father's money acuity, sense of responsibility or discernment in choosing friends.

When Humphrey came of age and received his inheritance, he was suddenly rich. No longer did he have to ask his mother for an allowance, or permission to entertain; he could do as he pleased. Humphrey never really believed that he would ever manage to spend the fortune that had been left to him and he took it as a challenge. Whatever the latest trend or fashion, Humphrey had to have it. He threw lavish parties, kept an excellent stable and was the soul of generosity with all his friends – of which, unsurprisingly, there were many.

His mother watched it all in despair, but there was little she could do. The older generation shook their heads in disapproval. Everyone talked of his wild ways and soon, whenever he was mentioned, he was no longer referred to as Humphrey Kynaston of Myddle, but as Wild Humphrey. The money melted away, like butter on a crumpet, and soon the coffers were almost empty.

When he realised how desperate things were, Humphrey finally listened to his mother. She arranged a match with a young woman from a good family and a dowry large enough to solve Humphrey's money worries. But Humphrey did not settle to family life as his mother had hoped. He went straight back to his old ways, neglecting his wife and duties. Soon he was in the same situation again. The bills were mounting up and there was no money to pay them. His wife left him and returned to her family, and his friends, once plentiful, dwindled away. The few friends that were left refused to help him, convinced it was throwing good money after bad.

Humphrey lost everything: the castle, his wealth, and all his fine possessions. At the last moment, he salvaged one favourite hunter and galloped from the stable as the Sheriff and his men came knocking at the door to take him to debtors' prison. Humphrey found shelter at Nescliff, in a cave carved out of the sandstone rock. It had two chambers, an inner one for him and an outer one for his horse. A stair of narrow steps carved into the stone led up to it.

Sitting in the cave, outlawed, Humphrey had plenty of time to think. There are whispers about those first dark days, when Humphrey felt hunger for the first time; days when despair gnawed at his soul and there seemed no escape from his debts, the Sheriff or a life of shame and dishonour. Rumours spread that he sold his soul to the Devil; that the spirit of the Devil entered his horse and would carry him out of all peril. The horse was named Beelzebub, and seeing the black stallion galloping at full speed, mane and tail flying behind it, white foam at its mouth, it was easy to believe that the Devil sped its hooves.

Others say it was the kindness of local families that helped him become what he was. They took pity on him, and instead of handing him over to the law, invited him into their homes, sharing their food with him. It was humble fodder of a type that Humphrey had never tasted, a far cry from all the luxurious delicacies he had served on his table. And yet, with hunger for sauce, it was the best food he had ever tasted.

Everyone agrees that Humphrey experienced poverty for the first time. He looked around with newly opened eyes and saw the great divide between rich and poor. He became a changed man and swore that he would do everything in his power to bring equality to all, to make the world a fairer place.

He didn't lose his flair for the dramatic. Humphrey Kynaston embarked on a career as a highwayman.

His former life had given him an insight into how and when the rents were collected. He soon worked out the favourite routes of the stewards and found it surprisingly easy to hold them up and relieve them of large sums of money. Humphrey never kept the money for himself, but shared it out amongst the local poor.

Humphrey quickly became a hero of the poor, but he was the bane of local landowners. They were all the more affronted because he had been one of them; most of them had shared a table with Humphrey's father. One of old Kynaston's greatest friends had been Mr Lloyd of Aston, but Humphrey was as happy to alleviate his pockets as anyone else's. Mr Lloyd was determined to be rid of Humphrey, the rotten apple in his friend's bloodline, and he offered large rewards for his capture. Humphrey was not impressed, though not surprised, how Mr

Lloyd had turned against him. Early one morning, he whistled
his horse, jumped on its back and set off for Aston Hall. He
arrived around noon and rode into his courtyard. He sent up
his name and a request for a few words with Mr Lloyd, who
could barely believe his ears; he rushed over to the window
and sure enough, there was Wild Humphrey waiting outside
his own front door.

Mr Lloyd emerged, all smiles, and politely invited
Humphrey in.

'Thank you, but no, I've urgent business and I'm short of time,' Humphrey returned. 'Still, I couldn't pass the house of such a good friend of my father's without calling in to give my regards. On the other hand, the road has put dust in my throat and I wouldn't say no to a draught of ale.'

A silver tankard was duly brought out and handed up to Humphrey, who drank to his host's health and then coolly slipped the tankard in his pocket. In the meantime, Mr Lloyd had signalled to his servants to close the gates. As the gates were closing, Humphrey nodded his head to Mr Lloyd, wheeled his horse around, sped towards the gates and leaped over both servants and gates to speed away into the distance.

Humphrey's life began to settle in to a routine. Every Sunday his mother would come to visit him in the cave and bring him his dinner. On Monday mornings, the local people would come and gather at his cave and he would share out all the money he had stolen in the week before. In return, they looked after Humphrey well. They brought food for him and his horse, made sure he had blankets to sleep under, clothes to wear and all of life's necessities. They helped keep his location a secret, and though the rewards proffered for his arrest grew greater and greater, none of the local poor ever tried to claim them. A farrier lived close to Humphrey's cave and he regularly reshod Beelzebub, sometimes with the shoes on backwards so a trail would lead in the opposite direction, sometimes with a cross, or with any one of a hundred different patterns, so that Humphrey's pursuers could not recognise his trail and follow it back to the cave.

Humphrey's horse, Beelzebub, was key to his success. The bond between horse and rider was uncanny; they seemed to think as one. When not riding him, Humphrey used to turn Beelzebub loose and whistle when he needed him again. Unbeknownst to Humphrey, Beelzebub had one favourite field where the grass must have been particularly sweet. Eventually, the farmer to whom the field belonged had had enough. Once or twice he might not have minded, but it seemed that every time he looked out at the field there was the great black beast munching on his best grazing. The next time it happened he called all his labourers together and equipped them with ropes to catch the stallion. They made a circle around the horse and slowly advanced towards him. The animal continued pulling at the grass, showing no sign of having noticed them. The circle tightened; Beelzebub grabbed a last few mouthfuls of grass, then lifted his head and headed toward one of the men, picking up speed. The man stood frozen to the ground, terrified, as Beelzebub thundered towards him. As the man cowered in fear, expecting to be trampled, Beelzebub leapt clear over him with a flick of his heels and was off, leaving the farmer swearing and the others watching in disbelief.

Another time, Humphrey was visiting the mother of one of the many families who had shown him kindness. She lay sick of a fever and he had brought her a basket of delicacies to tempt her appetite. While he was inside, a young lad saw Humphrey's horse wandering free and couldn't resist the temptation. He jumped up onto the back of Beelzebub, who allowed the lad to ride him away. When Humphrey came out of the cottage he whistled for his horse. Beelzebub pricked up his ears, bucked the lad high up into the air and cantered back to his master, leaving the would-be thief with a sore backside and a lesson learned.

Without the aid of Beelzebub, Humphrey's career as a highwayman would have been short-lived; Beelzebub's swift hooves outdistanced all pursuit and saved him from capture on almost a daily basis. Humphrey's horse was as notorious as Humphrey himself.

His most famous accomplishment came when they were in greatest peril. The well-to-do gentlemen of Shropshire joined forces with the Sheriff and they set a trap. They let it be overheard that a particularly plump purse was being transferred. Word reached Humphrey, as intended, and the messenger set off on the appointed day with a purse heavy with lead and a few coins on top. There was an obvious ambush point along

the road that they hoped Humphrey would use, and they lay
in wait for him. The steward, bearing the bait, arrived on the
road, and sure enough there was Humphrey, thundering along
on Beelzebub, grabbing the reins of the steward and taking the
heavy bag. A holler came from within the trees and twenty
gentlemen, on their best horses, rode towards Humphrey.
Beelzebub reared and turned and the chase began. The men
in pursuit fanned out into a half moon and herded Humphrey
towards the River Severn. Humphrey headed for Montford
Bridge, as his pursuers had hoped and expected. What
Humphrey did not know was that they had been there before
him and taken the planks from the middle of the bridge. Now
there was a yawning void that no horse could jump, with the
treacherous river down below. Humphrey's pursuers had him
surrounded from behind as he came to the bridge, and man
and horse saw the gap at the same time. Perhaps Humphrey
would have hesitated, but Beelzebub put on an extra spurt of
speed, kicked off from the remaining plank and soared over the
Severn, his pursuers watching open-mouthed in disbelief. His
hooves landed on the wood on the far side, scrabbling for pur-
chase, and then they were away, on the other side of the river.

The leap was so extraordinary that it was measured and
marked out on Knockin Heath with an 'H' and a 'K' cut into
the turf at the ends of the leap. The letters were renewed each
year and maintained for nearly two centuries.

One morning, Humphrey was sat outside his cave. It had
been a good week for him: he had claimed a rather splendid
haul, nearly six hundred pounds, from the steward of a large
estate, and distributed it on Monday as usual. The weather was
good and he was taking a moment to put his feet up. Through
the trees he saw movement. He tensed, then saw it was a lad
from the village.

'Morning, Robert. How fares the world with you today?'
he asked.

'Well, sir, thank you. I've brought you a letter,' replied the boy.

Intrigued, Humphrey took the letter and started to read.

A thoughtful frown developed as he read the letter, then read it again. The letter was from the owner of the estate whose rents he had stolen the week before. He claimed that the robbery had put him into dire straits. He would now have to call in all arrears due from his tenants, enforcing payment from families in difficulty; families he would normally allow time to get back on their feet.

Humphrey jumped to his feet and paced up and down the clearing in front of his cave. At last he stopped and turned to the lad.

'You brought this letter to me; I assume that you can return a letter to the gentleman?'

Robert nodded his head.

Humphrey quickly penned a reply, asking the gentleman for a list of tenants, so that he could find out if he really was the benign landlord he claimed to be.

The estate owner happily supplied the list and Humphrey made enquiries. To his surprise, the landlord was indeed much respected by all his tenants. In fact, he couldn't find anyone with a bad word to say about him. That is, none of his tenants – some of the other landlords were less complimentary.

On hearing the reports, Humphrey determined that he must repay the money as soon as possible. However, he had already shared the money out. As he pondered this new quandary, the answer arrived – a report that a Shrewsbury landlord, with an estate near Oswestry, had just given orders to his stewards to call in all the rents that were due, regardless of circumstance, from all his tenants on the estate. Humphrey lay in wait for the steward on his way back to Shrewsbury. The steward didn't stand a chance, and in moments the clanking bags were light once more, though he had heavy news to carry to his master.

Humphrey met the honest landlord in a wood near Old Oswestry and repaid the exact amount to the farthing.

Humphrey never was captured. In fact, eventually he was pardoned. Even so, he stayed in the cave to the end. During one of his visits to the sick he caught a fever, and as he lay, pale and sweating, there was a constant stream of visitors bringing soups, syrups, blankets and balms. In his fever he talked of his former life, of his friends and extravagances, of how he had been as bad, or worse, than many of the landowners he now punished. Most of all, he talked about his wife, the woman who had come into his home, bringing her fortune and dreams with her, and how he had used and ignored her.

There was an old woman in West Felton, renowned for her knowledge of herbs and healing skills. A group of the local women brought her to the cave to try and help Humphrey. The wise lady shooed all the attendants out of the cave and sat on the pallet next to Humphrey, laying a cool hand on Humphrey's brow. Humphrey's coughs racked his body; he caught his breath and weakly pushed her hand away, saying:

> Save your skills for someone you can cure. I do not think I can recover from this. It is not just my body that is ill, but my mind. While I lie here I am tormented by my past, by thoughtless, selfish things that I have done, by the memory of a beautiful woman whose life I ruined with my reckless behaviour. If I could see her once more…if she would bless me with her forgiveness…then I could rest easy at last.

The old woman sat up straight. The crookedness fell away as she slipped the cloak from her hair and shoulders. Humphrey looked at her in amazement as he saw that the old woman was no old woman at all, but his own wife.

'You are not the same man I married. You have proved yourself since coming to this cave. I forgave you a long time ago,' she smiled.

Humphrey smiled back up at her. His wild nature stopped fighting. His mind eased and he fell into a deep and restful sleep. His wife stayed with him and nursed him through his last few days, and when he died he went peacefully, holding her hand with a smile on his face.

As for Beelzebub, he was nowhere to be found.

IPPIKIN

Ippikin was a robber knight, a highway thief without mercy. Any money he took stayed within his own purse. He was dark haired, dark eyed, dark hearted. Some said that he was a knight's son, disinherited for his cruelty; some said that he was a magician who could renew his youth every seventy years; some said that he had struck a bargain with the Devil. People said a lot of things, but they said them in whispers, looking over their shoulders.

Ippikin and his band of robbers held sway over the Edge and all the local area. Travellers making their way along the Edge grouped together for safety, huddling close and travelling fast, hoping that Ippikin and his band were safely in their cave counting their hoard of gold and jewels, rather than lying in wait behind the trees.

Ippikin's reign of fear seemed never-ending and inescapable, until one night there was an almighty storm. The air crackled, the sky was torn and the earth shuddered as huge trees toppled. Ippikin and his men sheltered in their lair, a cave on the steep side of the Edge. A bolt of lightning seared the cliff above them and a mass of overhanging rock slid down the cliff-side, blocking the entrance and trapping them, leaving them buried in the cave with their gold.

But Ippikin is still there in that cave — a dark, malevolent presence brooding within the Edge. Anyone foolish enough can still summon Ippikin's spirit by standing on Ippikin's Rock, which protrudes above Ippikin's cave, and saying, 'Ippikin, Ippikin, keep away with your long chin!'

Dark haired, dark eyed, dark hearted: his thick gold chain still about his neck, he appears to hurl his summoner over the precipice.

Three

A County Divided

Major's Leap

Major's Leap, on Wenlock Edge, commands a panoramic view of Shropshire towards Cheshire and Wales. There is a very steep drop!

During the Civil War, Shrewsbury, Bridgnorth and Ludlow were all Royalist strongholds. One of the King's most loyal supporters, Major Thomas Smallman, lived on Wenlock Edge at Wilderhope Manor.

Although many were loyal to the King, the Parliamentary forces were gathering ranks. While Major Smallman was away discussing tactics at Bridgnorth, Wilderhope was sacked by Cromwellian supporters. The Major arrived home to find the doors open, his pewter, silver and everything of value taken, all else discarded and broken. He stayed only long enough to saddle fresh horses for himself and his small band of followers, and to hear in which direction the looters had gone. They caught up with the Roundheads near Ludlow. Before the Roundheads knew what was happening the Royalists were amongst them. Although Major Smallman was outnumbered by nearly ten to one, the looters never stood a chance. When the slaughter was done, he reclaimed his belongings and rode home, leaving the bodies where they had fallen.

Word spread amongst both sides. Already well respected by the King's supporters, the tale, growing in each retelling, made Major Smallman a hero. The Parliamentarians heard of a cold-blooded killer, a man who treated the dead with contempt, a figurehead to be destroyed. They wanted revenge. Major Smallman was watched closely.

The Roundheads' opportunity came when Major Smallman was riding secretly from Bridgnorth to Shrewsbury, with plans for a large-scale attack tucked inside his shirt. Cromwell's men set up an ambush. Major Smallman was surrounded and this time he was overpowered. Trussed up like a Christmas goose, they tied him onto his horse. Laughing and celebrating, the Roundheads led him back to his own manor and imprisoned him in his own room, but they did not discover the hidden plans. The Roundheads made themselves comfortable down-stairs, ordering the frightened servants to bring out the finest food Smallman's larder and cellar could provide. In his room Major Smallman could hear them laughing and feasting as they discussed what to do with him. Some were for executing him immediately, hanging him outside his own manor. Others had something more public in mind; the Major should stand trial for his crimes and be publicly put to death where the Royalist supporters could see his humiliation.

The Major was locked up behind a oak door, a sentry standing guard. What his captors didn't know was that there was another way out of the Major's room: a hidden passage from the fireplace, a spiral staircase down to the kitchen, winding between the chim-ney and the outside wall. The Major crept down the stairs and, peering into the kitchen, waited for his moment. While some of the servants distracted the guard set to watch over them, a kitchen maid bustled him outside. The Major ducked down beneath the windows and headed to the stables at the back of the manor.

The first inkling of his escape came with the sound of hooves, then a fleeting glimpse of horse and rider racing past the window. The Roundheads raised the alarm, unlocking the Major's room to find it empty.

Major Smallman had a start on his pursuers and he knew the Edge better than anyone. He raced out across the fields, through Easthope woods, following the rise of the Edge. But the Roundheads were soon close behind him and gaining, whilst his own horse was tiring. He twisted and turned through the trees, ducking below low branches, hoping to unseat the enemies on his heels. But while he tried to shake off the pursuit behind him, others rode ahead to outflank him. Determined to keep the plans secret, and faced with public trial and hanging, the Major decided instead to die like a hero. He turned his horse's head and rode straight for the Edge. The trees thinned and he had one glimpse of the Shropshire plain laid out before him. He dug his spurs into his horse's flanks; the animal bunched its muscles and stretched out into a great leap over the cliff. For a moment they hung there, suspended in the air, then horse and rider fell flailing downward. The horses behind swerved and reared to avoid following them.

Peering over the Edge, the Roundheads saw the broken body of the horse far below. There was no way that the Major

could have survived the leap. Slowly they turned and headed home.

But miraculously, the Major survived. Caught in the branches of a crab-apple tree, his fall was broken. He held still, not believing his luck and barely breathing, until he heard the soldiers leave, and then cautiously clambered down the tree and the Edge.

Much later, a bruised and battered figure limped up to the Shrewsbury Garrison. Triumphantly Major Smallman handed over the plans and his story.

The Garrison sprang into action and a force was despatched, Major Smallman among them, to Wilderhope. The Roundheads cowered as Major Smallman burst in, a ghost on horseback. Revenge and triumph ran like fire through the Major's veins. The battle was over almost instantly, the Roundheads unprepared and too surprised to defend themselves. When all was secured, the Major crumpled like a rag doll, but there was a fierce smile on his face and he was lord of his own manor once more.

THE LOST BELLS OF COLEMERE

A riddle:

I saw five birds all in a cage
Each bird had but a single wing
They were a hundred years of age
And yet did fly and sweetly sing
The wonder did my mind possess
When I beheld their age and strength
Besides as near as I can guess
Their tails were thirty feet in length

Colemere is a beautiful mere tucked away in a quiet corner of North Shropshire, between the hamlets of Colemere and Lyneal. The Victorian church stands by the road on the high ground, looking over the meadow and reed beds that lead down to the mere. Trees border the rest of the mere, bowing down to admire themselves in the still water. The water is sheltered, rarely ruffled by the wind. In the summer, water lilies with tiny yellow flowers float on the top of the water, belying how deep the water really is. It is a still, contemplative place, changing with the seasons, but not the years.

Before the new church was built, there was a chapel much closer to the water. Follow the path down through the meadow, through the kissing gate and into the woods. If you explore to your right, you can still find an ancient yew tree, cloistered among the younger trees. It is the last marker and guardian of the old chapel site now that the bricks and mortar of St Helen's are long gone.

In the time of the Civil War, Shropshire, like all of England, lay divided. Shrewsbury and the South were mostly loyal to the King, but Oswestry, Whitchurch and the North supported Cromwell. There was unrest throughout the county and neighbours looked at one another with mistrust.

Amongst the common folk, support for Cromwell was swelling, more and more people being swayed by the radical new ideas. One night, things came to a head in Lyneal. A mass gathering of men and women, many disguised, rioted through the village, and at last converged on the banks of Colemere at St Helen's Chapel. They came shouting and hollering with torches and ropes, throwing stones and rocks. The mob pulled the chapel down, wrecking the building and throwing the bells into the mere. But the bells did not lie quiet. On windy nights, when the moon was full, the bells would sound beneath the water.

Years later, in quieter times, the local people decided to try and reclaim the bells. They asked the local henwife for help.

'Twenty oxen you'll need and a good deal of respect. Those bells are calling out to be lifted, but mind your tongues while you pull. Go in silence and solemnity and the bells will be glad to come home.'

As in earlier times, opinion was again divided. Not everyone thought it was a good idea to raise the bells, and not everyone was

the Bells are pulled up from the Lake

sure they'd manage it. However, there were plenty of willing volunteers to try and bring the bells to shore. And so men and women from Colemere and Lyneal gathered together in silence and solemnity. Some young lads swam down to the bells with chains and fastened them tight. Twenty oxen were harnessed to the chains and they began to pull. The oxen began to move and there was a swell in the water. Higher and higher the bells were lifted, closer and closer to the shore, until just as they crested the water, a man turned to one of the more vocal dissenters of the effort and whispered, 'You see! After all your doubts, in spite of God and the Devil, we have done it!'

As soon as the words were out of his mouth, the chains snapped. The bells rolled back into the water, rattling the chains behind them, sinking deeper this time, down to the heart of the mere.

The people stood watching the bubbles rise where the bells had sunk, but there was nothing that could be done. The bells were beyond the reach of human divers. No more do the bells toll beneath water; no more do they cry to come home; now they lie still, silent in the depths.

THE WOMEN OF WEM

Lord Capel, King Charles' man through and through, waited for dawn, savouring the moment. In a few hours, victory, fame and the King's heartfelt gratitude would all be his. Wem was his for the taking as soon as the sun lit the way; its defences unfinished and its protectors lured away to Nantwich. Wem was the first town in Shropshire to declare for Parliament and, once Lord Capel had stamped out the uprising, he was determined it would be the last.

Lord Capel had not been in Shropshire long. When the King heard of the new garrison at Wem, he sent Lord Capel with a new title: Lieutenant-General of Shropshire, Cheshire, and North Wales. His main role was to combat Sir William Brereton, Commander-in-Chief of Parliamentary forces in Cheshire.

Lord Capel knew that Wem was building its defences and realised he needed to take the town before it completed its preparations. He also knew that Sir Brereton's men were gathered at Wem to prevent him from doing just that.

Lord Capel had gathered a force of nearly 5,000 men with arms and provisions. But instead of attacking Wem, he had taken a small number of his troops to Nantwich. They attacked and looted several of the outlying villages, then set fire to Nantwich itself, Lord Capel making certain he was seen and recognised. As dusk fell they lit hundreds of campfires, making it look as if an army was camped just outside Nantwich. In the darkness, the Royalists left their fires burning and raced back to Shropshire. As Lord Capel had planned, Nantwich sent distress calls to Lord Brereton in Wem, who took his army to defend what for many of them was their home town.

Lord Capel galloped back to his main force and marched it onto Wem's doorstep. It was to be the perfect battle. Most of his troops had never tasted action before. Wem would give them an easy victory, the confidence they would need for the war ahead.

On the other side of the ramparts a messenger raised the alarm. The few soldiers left were inclined to agree with Lord Capel; only forty soldiers were left to defend the garrison, with the ramparts unfinished, the gate unhinged and precious few weapons or ammunition. A message was sent to Lord Brereton for support, but they knew he could not return in time. There was nothing they could do.

The women of the Wem saw the slumped shoulders of the men that were supposed to be protecting them and were not impressed. They would not admit defeat before the battle had even begun. They ransacked the town, gathering every broomstick, pot, pan and cauldron they could find – anything that might be of use. The soldiers watched in bemusement as the pile of domestic utensils piled higher and girls began polishing the cooking pots with soot and lampblack.

The soldiers averted their eyes as the women reached under their skirts to pull off their red woollen petticoats. Each woman wrapped her petticoat around her shoulders, then found a broom handle to hold as a musket. The watching men groaned as the women lined up and practised a soldier's stance. Not only were the soldiers to be defeated, but humiliated in the process. They could already imagine the taunts: needing their mothers

to hold their hands on the battlefield or being so henpecked that the women fought their battles for them.

A few of the older townswomen came over to the soldiers. 'If you stood up and fought like men, instead of planning your defeat, we might just stand a chance. There's not much time left.'

The captain didn't see much hope, but at least the women were busy rather than panicking. He ordered his men to humour them, and together they mounted the pots and cauldrons like cannons on top of the ramparts. The women stood as sentries all around the ramparts.

The sun rose and the long night was over. With a cheer, Lord Capel sent his army forward to attack, his soldiers giving a great shout as they ran towards Wem. Lord Capel lit his pipe to watch the victory. But as his troops broke cover and approached the town, they saw red-coated soldiers atop the walls, taking aim with their guns. The early morning sun glinted off the polished cannons. Lord Capel's new recruits had been promised an easy victory, but now they found themselves exposed on open ground, muskets and cannon bearing down on them. The few arms that the town possessed all fired towards the invading forces and several Cavaliers fell. That was enough; the Royalists turned tail and fled. Lord Capel stood on the battlefield, pipe still in hand, begging his troops to stay and fight, while up on the ramparts the women danced and cheered.

When at last Lord Brereton returned to Wem, he was stunned to find the town unbreached and Lord Capel's forces long gone on the road to Shrewsbury. When Brereton heaped praise upon the soldiers left behind, they were forced to admit that the victory was won by the women. The story spread amongst Parliamentary forces everywhere; the Roundheads celebrated their women and Cavaliers throughout the country were forced to endure the taunt:

> The women of Wem and a few musketeers
> Beat the Lord Capel and all his Cavaliers.

Four

WILY WOMEN AND THE DEVIL'S BREW

BETTY FOX AND THE TREASURE

Betty Fox was a wheelwright's wife and she lived at Wroxeter. Long gone were the days when she was 'Beautiful Betty' or 'Betty the Belle'; now they called her 'Old Mother Fox'. Long gone too was the first flush of love and romance, though she and her husband muddled along together well enough. He worked hard doing his best to provide for them and she'd brought up a whole brood of children. But Betty was tired of being poor. She'd had enough of scraping by and making do. She dreamed of going into Shrewsbury to buy herself a new dress, of cooking steak and onions, of her neighbours looking at her in admiration once again.

Betty lived not far from the ruins at Wroxeter, where they said there was once a great and beautiful city, though there was little more than buried rubble there now. Every now and then, people digging their taters or out ploughing would turn up an old coin from the city. Betty's eyes had always been sharp and they hadn't dimmed with age. Whenever she was out and about, she would keep a look out. She'd walk with a stick, swishing down the nettles and poking amongst the brambles, just in case.

One night, Betty was sound asleep, dreaming she was walking towards Wroxeter down Horseshoe Lane. She was swishing her stick as she walked along and something caught her eye. There was a big alder bush growing out of the bank by the side of the lane. The ground beneath the alder cracked open, white light spilling out of the crack. Inside, nestled in the earth, she could see a pile of silver coins shining. Betty reached down to pick up one of the coins, but just as she was about to take it in her hand, she woke up.

'Husband!' she cried, 'Husband, wake up! I've just had the most wonderful dream! There was a beautiful light and so many silver coins…'

'You daft old besom!' he said, 'What are you doing, waking me up in the middle of the night with your flights of fancy. Go back to sleep and let me do the same.' He rolled over, pulled the blankets over his head and soon the room reverber-ated to the sound of his snoring once more.

Betty took a little longer to go back to sleep. At last her breathing slowed and there she was, back on the lane, walk-ing towards Wroxeter. There was the alder bush. The ground parted beneath the tree. She could see the tree roots and the silver pool of coins gleaming white. She reached out to touch them and found herself back in her bed.

'Oh, I saw it again – a big pile of beautiful coins and I know just the place! Oh husband, husband, put on your clothes and let's go and have a look.'

'You foolish old woman! That's twice you've woken me now. If you don't let me sleep I won't be in a fit state to earn any real coins tomorrow and I don't think the rent man will take your pretty dream coins to pay for the roof over our head. For pity's sake, go to sleep!'

As soon as Betty closed her eyes she was back on Horseshoe Lane. She was standing in front of the alder bush and looking at the silver coins cradled between the roots. As she bent down

to pick one up, she started awake in the bed. Her husband was still snoring.

'Well now,' thought Betty, 'There's power in dreams and there's power in threes. If you dream the same dream three times, you'd be a fool to ignore it, my girl!' Betty crept out of bed and grabbed a shawl to wrap around her shoulders. She found her walking stick and a spade. The moon was nearly full and her silvery light lit Betty's way as she walked down the lane. At last, she saw the silhouette of the alder in the hedge. She sliced the ground with the spade and started to dig. It wasn't long before the spade shattered an old earthenware pot and silver coins spattered out. Betty could barely believe her eyes. She scooped up handful after handful and hurried home with her apron full.

When she reached home, she saw a light in the kitchen. There was her husband sat at the table with a candle, woken by the cold, empty bed. Before he could ask where she'd been, she put a tuppeny dish on the table and let all the silver coins pour into it.

'Well, fool or no fool, I've found the treasure!' she exclaimed. Her husband's eyes grew round and he pulled his wife into his arms.

Betty and her husband sold the coins and it's said she made as much as thirty pounds for them. She put away her walking stick and put on a new dress. When she walked down the lane, the spring in her step and sparkle in her eyes were enough to make all the neighbours' heads turn.

NELLIE IN THE CHURCHYARD

If on my theme I rightly think
There are five reasons why men drink:
Good wine, a friend, because I'm dry,
Or else I should be by and by,
Or any other reason why.

Dr Henry Aldrich, D.D. (1647-1710) Rector of Wem

Oh! It had been a good market day. Old Nellie's hens were doing well that summer – they'd had so many chicks and all of them had survived and were growing strong. All but the few mother hens were laying an egg a day and a double yolk as often as not. She'd had dozens of eggs to take to Wem market. She'd sold them all, at a good price too, and filled her pockets with jingling coins. The town had been buzzing that day; the sun shone, all the stalls were teeming with people, there were buskers and tumblers entertaining the crowds, and business was good for everyone. Nowhere was business better than in the alehouses and inns, and there were plenty to choose from: the Bulls Head, Bucks Head, Beehive and Brass Knocker; the Pheasant, Pack Horse and Painters' Arms; the Swan and the Seven Stars, the Grove Inn, Royal Oak Inn, Crown Inn and the Dickin Arms. The sunshine and banter brought out the thirst in everyone, and that included old Nellie.

'I'll just have a little sup to clear the dust from my throat,' thought Nellie. The first one slipped down so easily that a second swiftly followed. The company and conversation were like water on parched earth after talking to no one but her chickens all week. With all that talking, her throat was soon parched too, and the remedy was close at hand.

When Nellie made her way out of the alehouse, the sun had gone and so had the jingle in her pockets. Nellie had no thought of walking home that night and no money to pay for somewhere to stay. It was a mild evening and anyway, Nellie was warm from the beer. She carefully swayed her way down the street toward the churchyard – it would not be the first time she'd slept there on a market night.

'Well, Nellie, old girl, you're not getting any younger, you might as well get to know your future neighbours,' she'd smile to herself whenever she bedded down there. Nellie knew a good spot. There was a big slab – a mausoleum with the sides fallen in – a good size for Nellie to snuggle down under to keep her safe from any drunken jokers and night time show-ers. Nellie slipped in under the big stone, as she'd often done before, and soon she was fast asleep.

Nellie wasn't the only one who'd been enjoying the market day atmosphere. There were a fair few people coming out of the alehouses as, one by one, they closed their doors for the night. Their singing and laughter drifted over the churchyard wall as they passed by. A group of lads over from Clive for the day were not yet ready to finish their night's carousing. They piled out of the alehouse with a big jug of beer and looked for somewhere to carry on their drinking: the churchyard seemed the perfect place.

'I doubt we'll disturb the dreams of any of these sleepers!' laughed one of the lads. They spotted the flat slab, a perfect table for them to gather around. The jug passed from one to another as the night wore on. There came a lull in the talk and, into the quiet, the church bells tolled the midnight hour. A chill struck the five young men, a brief sober moment, then one lad, with a wink to his companions, took up the ale jug and said, 'Now then, what rude guests we are! Here's our man, hosting us so kindly at his table and we've not even offered him a drink!' His companions laughed as he bent down, holding the jug by the grave.

From underneath the stone stretched out a bent and wizened hand, a skinny arm following, reaching up to take the jar.

The five Clive lads leapt up to their feet and backed away from the arm that cradled their beer as it drew the jar into the grave. As one, they turned and fled, fear speeding their feet, all traces of merriment gone in an instant. The young men

raced home to Clive faster than they'd ever travelled the route before. The next day they were swift to tell of their supernatural encounter.

Old Nellie drank the ale appreciatively and slept well and long afterwards. She woke with a smile the next day, and she too told her story to anyone who would listen – and earned herself several drinks for the telling of it. With a mischievous twinkle in her eye, she claimed she'd like every night to be mistook for a corpse!

Oh, but when the two stories met, there were red faces in Clive and it was a long time before the Clive lads came back to market in Wem.

THE WENLOCK DEVIL

In the 1800s, Much Wenlock had a reputation for hard drinking. When Reverend Wayne was appointed Vicar of Wenlock, he wrote to the Town Clerk, Humphrey Hinton, to ask whether the society, the roads and the water were good. Mr Hinton replied that the society and the roads were fine, but stated that he 'could give no information about the water as the Wenlock people never drank it'!

To refuse a drink was a grave insult and led to a reputation as a 'mean-spirited milksop'. When the Temperance Movement first reached Much Wenlock, it was greeted with disbelief. Doctor William Penny Brookes, the man responsible for reviving the Olympics, was on a one-man mission to improve the moral, intellectual and physical well-being of the people of Wenlock, and was a supporter of the Temperance Movement. When Dr Brookes was elected a hereditary burgess at a dinner in the Raven Hotel, he was expected to toast 'Prosperation to the Corporation' and down the contents of the mace. When Dr Brookes refused to empty the silver cup, an incredulous mutter went around the table. One of the leading officials rose to his feet, warning, 'Doctor, Doctor, don't disgrace yourself!'

In the early days of the movement, a temperance preacher came to give a sermon in Much Wenlock. He preached the evils of the Devil's brew, of drunkenness leading to quarrels between brothers, and emptying the pockets of the hard-working man. As the sermon continued, a large proportion of the congregation began to feel rather aggrieved at the slur they felt the minister was laying on their characters, all God-fearing, church-attending men who saw nothing wrong with slaking their thirst after a hard day's work. The resentment and muttering grew, until one man called out, 'Get down and make room for a better man!'

The clerk, sexton and churchwarden were sent to eject the heckler. As they surrounded him, the man stood up, dwarfing the three churchmen as he towered over them. He was nearly as broad as he was tall, and strong as an ox from working in the quarries. The churchmen found themselves flying through the air and out the door, rather than the other way around. After that the meeting dissolved into a free for all; some took the side of the quarryman, others the side of the preacher. Fists and feet flailed out from all sides and no one knew quite how they managed to get the preacher home safely. The mob rioted through the town, no doubt fuelled with some of the Devil's brew. Windows were broken through the town and then the mob took the town stocks, hurled them inside a limekiln and burnt them with much cheering and singing.

The burning of the stocks did not mean that the rioting offenders went unpunished. A new set of stocks was commissioned specifically to punish the miscreants, and the new design was made with wheels. The constables thought the new stocks were marvellous, as they could wheel the stocks around town to take the miscreant wherever would get the largest audience and greatest humiliation. However, the members of the mob did not seem to feel much shame; in fact, they delighted in the wheels as much as the constables. The people of the town generally sided with the rioters and brought them ale from the nearest alehouse, turning the punishment into something more akin to a pub crawl. The last to be punished was a man from Broseley known as 'Snailey'. When Snailey was released he said he had been 'treated like a real lord' and he felt as if he 'was going straight to Heaven'. It was commonly agreed that he was more drunk after the day in the stocks than on the night of the riot.

Such was the atmosphere when the new temperance minister and his family came to Wenlock. The minister had been warned about the attitude of the town. He was resigned to a slow and quiet start, confident that his message was strong enough to be heard eventually. He knew his congregation would be small, but there was an unexpected worshipper to swell his numbers. There at the back, face shiny and scrubbed, clothes tidy and clean, was Bill. As far as anyone knew, Bill had never been to a church service before unless it was a wedding, funeral or baptism, and only a handful of those. On the other hand, Much Wenlock was a town of inns and alehouses – the Plough, Raven, Royal Oak, George, Talbot, Swan and Falcon, Stork, Fox, Railway Tavern, White Hart and Horse and Jockey – and Bill was a devout follower of them all.

The next week, Bill still went out drinking every night, until it came to Saturday, when he stayed sober and was back at the service on Sunday. At the end of the service, the reason for Bill's sudden change of heart became clear. Shuffling from foot to foot, red-faced, Bill nervously made his way over to Esther, the minister's daughter.

'May I walk you home, Miss Esther, please?'

Esther was tall and slender with glossy dark hair. She was eighteen or nineteen, a decade younger than Bill and a world apart in their daily lives. Her mouth dropped open in surprise, giving her father a moment to step over to her side. Esther was just forming her refusal when her father said, 'Of course you may, William, and thank you for your kind offer.'

Esther's mouth opened and closed like a fish out of water, looking at her father in bemusement, but she proffered her arm and Bill walked her the short distance to her home, her parents following a little way behind.

Bill took his leave of Esther at the gate, with a promise to see her the next Sunday. The minister took his daughter inside and sat her down.

'Esther, you've been given a chance to do a great thing. You've inspired that man to try a new way of life. And if we can convert Bill, a confirmed drunkard, to our cause, then who knows what we can achieve! All I'm asking is for a little kindness and charity. Let him walk you home and tell him about the church.'

Well, there were certain young men in the town that Esther would have much preferred to walk her home, but she agreed and did what her father asked. The following Sunday, Bill was sat in the service again, and at the end he made his way over to Esther with a shy smile. Esther forced a smile in return and her father nodded approval.

Over the following weeks and months, the Sunday routine became established. Bill would scrub himself up, sit attentively through the service and afterwards walk Esther the short way down the street to her home, always within view of her parents, of course. Esther would talk to him of how her father had been inspired to become a minister, about the Temperance Movement and what it had achieved. Bill was completely besotted. He was still too tongue-tied to find much to say to her, but he was content to walk beside her, drinking in her voice, her laugh, her scent, the way her hair caught the sun. Bill had almost stopped drinking altogether. He was carefully hoarding his wages, saving all the money he would usually spend on ale. He was saving for a ring.

One Saturday, he got his pay packet and the last few pence needed to buy the ring he had been saving for. He went straight into town and handed over his money, then put on his Sunday best a day early, plucked up his courage and knocked on the minister's door. The family were surprised to see him, but he was ushered in. In front of Esther's parents, he took her hand, brought out the ring and asked, if her parents would give their permission, would she marry him?

The answer was written all too plainly across Esther's face. Instead of the affection and pleasure he had dared to imagine, shock, dismay and disgust raced in quick succession across her face. She snatched her hand away as though she had been burnt.

Colour flushed from Bill's collar up into his cheeks. His face clouded over with hurt, then humiliation and anger. He turned and stumbled from the room. The minister tried to follow, calling his name, but Bill brushed the minister's hand from his shoulder and escaped out into the street.

Bill made his way to the nearest alehouse and started drinking. He shrugged off the welcoming comments and offers of conversation, and when the other customers saw the grim look on his face, they left him alone with his beer. Bill visited all his old haunts that night, drinking his way through every inn, hotel and alehouse in the town, making no differentiation between gin and ale.

The next morning Esther was found dead in her bed. Her face was as pale as the pillow she lay on, her sheets stained crimson, red petals blooming around the knife sunk into her heart.

Her family were quick to name Bill as the murderer and the police were called. The murderer had climbed to the window and prised it open. The catch was broken; there was soil on the bedroom floor and, in the flowerbed outside the window, a perfect boot print in the soft earth.

It wasn't long before the police were banging on Bill's door. He was still in a stupor, sleeping off the alcohol of the night before. They dragged him from his bed and down to the cells. Bill remembered Esther's refusal and starting to drink, but with each alehouse the night grew hazier and he had no memory of getting home. An over zealous policeman took Bill's boot, hurried to the minister's house, pressed the boot into the print and declared it matched exactly. Of course, once he pressed the boot into the print, the soft earth moulded to the shape of Bill's boot and the original print was obliterated. But everyone

was sure that Bill had done
it; there was no other sus-
pect, no one else with
a motive.

She slept on the ground floor

The case came
quickly to trial.
Plenty of people
had seen Bill
around the
town that night,
and testified to
the grim mood
he was in and his
drunken state, but
no one had seen
Bill anywhere near
the minister's house. In
fact, although there was a strong motive, there was
no evidence against him at all. The only thing linking him
to the scene of the crime was the boot print, but now there
was no proof it was Bill's boot. The judge had no choice but
to direct the jury to find the defendant 'not guilty'. After the
verdict was read out, Bill stood up in court, looked around at
the accusing stares and said, 'If I did this foul deed, may the
Devil take me.'

Bill was set free, but Much Wenlock was an uncomfortable
place for him. Everyone knew the story and everyone thought
he'd done it. When Bill went into any alehouse, even if he
managed to get served, no one would share a table with him.

The minister's wife, desperate with grief for her child, stopped
going to worship with her husband, unable to pray to the
God who had taken her daughter. Instead, she went to Nanny
Morgan, up on Westwood Common. Nanny sold blessings and
curses, love potions and vengeance. Nanny Morgan used the
bible in a very different way than the minister's wife ever had;
she used psalms to ill-wish people. It was said that, 'When a

psalm was read by such a curser as Nanny Morgan, there was no angel in Heaven could flit by safe.' More than once Bill found himself looking into Nanny's steel-grey eyes, her voice knifing into him as the curses rained down.

Bill was forced to leave town. He moved away to Wolverhampton and got a job in a carding mill. It was only a few months later that word filtered back to Much Wenlock that he had been killed in an industrial accident by a piece of machinery known as 'the flying devil'.

NANNY MORGAN

Up on the Edge, at Westwood Common, was a house. Two dogs sat by the gate, watching everyone and everything that passed. On the roof, yellow eyes gleamed down from the cats, still as sentries. The windows were dark, no hint to the outside world of what might lie inside.

A girl stood undecided on the road, fiddling with her petticoats. She had walked up from town to this place, but now her heart failed her. Inside lived Nanny Morgan; old Nanny with eyes like steel, that could carve you open to rummage through your darkest secrets. Nanny Morgan – they said she'd been a beauty in her day – but you'd never know it now to look at her, with her bent back, hooked nose and thin hair. They said she'd run off with the gypsies when she was young, that they'd taught her how to read cards and tell fortunes. When she came back, she looked like she did now. A lot of people said that Nanny had wanted more than just playing with cards, and she'd been taught all those spells and curses by Someone Else; Someone that had taken her youth and beauty and had a seat by the fire, warmed and waiting for her. Everyone was frightened of Nanny.

The girl swallowed. Now here she was, practically on the old witch's doorstep. She took a deep breath and smoothed down her skirts; she'd come here for a reason.

Two dogs sat still BY THE gate

The girl walked to the gate. One of the dogs slunk away into the house, the other stared at the visitor and its lip curled just enough for her not to come any closer. A moment later a sharp bark came from the house, the gate opened and the dog lay down. The girl walked through the gate and up to the door. The door was ajar. She pushed it open and stepped inside. 'Hello?' she called, tentatively. The girl's voice quavered unanswered on the air.

The house smelt. Cats, definitely, and smoke, but something else too; something sour and strange. Slowly the girl's eyes adjusted to the gloom. There was paper everywhere, piles of letters and books. Her eye was drawn to a box in the corner. In the dim light, she could have sworn she saw it move. She crept over and peered inside. For a moment, her eyes couldn't decipher what she saw, then she realised that the box was full of toads, crawling one on top of the other, all trying to reach the top. Something warm and soft brushed the girl's leg.

'Oh!' she jumped. It was just a cat, now twining itself about her ankles.

'So…what do you want?!' The girl looked up to find Old Nanny staring unblinking at her.

'I…I…I've come for my future read…I've brought money.'

'And why do you want your fortune read? Have you been jilted? Deceived? Betrayed? No — I can see there's nothing budding in your belly. So…?'

'I…I've been offered marriage. But my heart lies another way. I want…I need to know if the one I love loves me.'

Nanny Morgan said nothing, but sat down at a little table, gesturing the girl to do the same. The old woman took the cards in her crabbed hands, shuffled them and laid them out on the table, one by one. The girl sat tensely, starting every time the fire popped in the grate. Nanny pondered the cards, then the girl. She slowly shook her head and said:

No. The one you love does not love you. He loves none but his own self. The marriage…that's a good offer. You should think about it. But be warned! When the one your heart desires sees you with another, he'll come courting with all his sweet words and if you listen, then once the chase is done, once he has won you, he will be gone and you will be left with neither lover nor suitor, nothing but a broken name.

The girl put her coin down on the table, nodded her head and was gone as soon as she could get out of the house. The old woman watched her go with a shrug of her shoulders and a shake of her head. She knew all too well her words had changed nothing.

Five

Foxes, Hounds
and the Wild Hunt

Tom Moody

> You all knew Tom Moody, the whipper-in well,
> The bell just done tolling was honest Tom's knell,
> A more able sportsman ne'er follow'd a hound,
> Thro' a country well known to him fifty miles round,
> No hound ever open'd with Tom near the wood,
> But he'd challenge the tone and could tell if 'twas good,
> And all with attention, would eagerly mark
> When he cheer'd up the pack, – 'Hark'!
> To Rockwood, hark! hark!
> High! wind Him! and cross him!
> Now Ratler, boy, hark!'

Tom was a small lad and would never be handsome after the pox
left his face pitted and pocked. But he was strong in a sinewy way,
and he was quick, stubborn and fearless. His eyes were bright; he
had a ready smile and was always up for a bit of mischief.

He was the son of a widow and had been needed to help
make ends meet as soon as he was able. He was apprenticed

to Adams the Malster and worked delivering the malt. One day he had delivered two sacks of malt and was on his way home, bareback on his master's cob. Tom thought there was no one about and set the cob at a gate. The horse laid its ears back, dug in its heels and refused to move, so Tom wheeled it around and tried again. He kept trying, keeping his seat and pushing the cob, until at last he persuaded the horse up and over. But someone had been watching.

George Forester, the squire, who happened to be riding that way, saw the first attempt and, his interest piqued, stayed until he saw the gate cleared. The squire was a man who loved horses and lived for the hunt. When he saw Tom, he saw a lad after his own heart. The squire made a few enquiries and, when he found out who the lad was, asked Adams the Malster if he would part with him. Well the Malster didn't mind, but when Tom's mother found her lad was wanted up at Willey Hall, she was terrified of what he might have done. She knew all too well the high spirited pranks her son was capable of. When she discovered that Tom was not in trouble at all, but instead had been offered a job by the squire himself, she was delighted.

Tom couldn't believe his luck. As the squire's stable lad his role was to care for the horses and ride out on errands. Tom worked hard and he had a knack with the horses. He had plenty of fun too; when his natural inclination for mischief led him astray, the squire did not punish him, but simply laughed and ruffled his hair. Tom didn't need a great deal of encouragement to push the boundaries.

Tom grew from a boy into a young man, his skill as a rider growing all the time, and he showed it off at every opportunity. With the squire's backing, and such beautiful horses available, he would take risks that no one else would dare.

Tom's jobs included driving the squire's buff-coloured chaise to take company home from the hall and collecting visitors from Shifnal, the nearest coaching post. He was always considerate with passengers, but once the gig was empty it was a different story. One time he was on the pike road, heading toward Shifnal at breakneck speed to catch the coach. The pike man was slow and did not come out to open the gate. Tom rode at a gallop to the gate and the horse reared to a halt in front of it. He stood waiting with his horse, fidgeting, until eventually the pike man appeared and Tom, now livid, gave the man a piece of his mind. The pike man said nothing, but he didn't hurry his step as he walked to the gate. When the gate was finally open, Tom was away at a gallop, leaving the man choking in a cloud of dust. Tom determined that he would not wait on the man the next time he headed that way. There were no words between them as Tom sedately brought his passengers back through the gate, but the next time the gig was empty, he urged the horse on as the gate loomed ahead of them. The pike man watched his coming, making no effort to speed his step. Tom did not slow down, but instead whipped the horse on. As they came to the gate, he urged the horse over, pulling the gig smoothly behind, barely losing rhythm as he came down on the far side and disappeared into the distance without paying his fee.

Tom tried the same trick the next time, but it didn't go quite so well. The horse sailed over, but one wheel of the gig caught on the top rail, flipping the gig and sending Tom up into the air and landing hard on his backside. The pike man burst out laughing and could only keep standing by clinging onto the gate.

'You know, I reckon that just about served you right!' he observed, wiping his eyes.

'You know, I think you might just be right!' replied Tom with a grin.

Tom lay flat on his back and laughed almost as hard as the pike man, until, in the end, the pike man walked over to Tom, held out a hand and hauled him to his feet. From that day on the two were firm friends. It didn't stop Tom from jumping over the gate now and then though, just for the sake of it!

The stables at Willey revolved around the hunt. As the days shortened, the excitement would build, the season looming closer and closer. The only way a boy like Tom ever got to hunt was by working in a stable such as George Forester's. At first he was only allowed on the sidelines, grooming the horses beforehand, cleaning them up afterwards and meeting the hunt with fresh horses. The squire knew how much Tom longed to join the hunt, and also what a good horseman he was. It wasn't long before Tom's skills were harnessed. Squire Forester gave him his pinks and made him whipper-in, his job being to keep the pack together and prevent the hounds from getting distracted by other scents.

Tom loved it. He made such a good whipper-in that he became famous throughout the county, and eventually beyond. (A whipper-in is only an assistant to the Master of the Hunt and rarely becomes known much outside his own hunt.) Tom's fame spread for three reasons. The first was that he was superb at his job. It was said that no one could keep a pack together, sustain the burst of a long chase and be in at the death, with every hound up with him, like Tom could.

The second was the way he rode. He had a horse that no one else would go near – an animal that was all teeth and hooves to anyone except him. But when Tom sat on him, the two would fly over wall, fence, ditch, brook or hedge – the higher and wider the better. The horse was huge, Tom was slight; when the two of them saw open country in front of them they would go from morning until night and think nothing of it.

The third reason was Tom's voice. Tom had a rich, clear, mellow tone that carried across acres. His 'halloo' to the hounds, his 'tally-ho' or his 'who-who-hoop', were so clear and melodic that they were often requested as a party piece in the pub, not just used in the field. One day Tom was recounting the adventures of the day's hunt in the servants' hall. He was in particularly fine voice and gave his 'who-who-hoop'. A moment later the housekeeper came bustling in and said, 'La! Tom, you have given the "who-who-hoop", as you call it, so very loud and strong today that you have set the cups and saucers a-dancing!'

One of the squire's guests, who had purposely placed himself within hearing to listen, replied, 'I am not at all surprised. His voice is music itself. I never heard anything so attractive and inspiring before in the whole course of my life; its tones are as fine and mellow as a French horn.'

Tom's voice saved his life at least once. He fell down an old pit shaft, the sides gave way and he was trapped with no way to get out. Tom gave his 'halloo' to the hounds. It reverberated out of the shaft mouth and carried over the fields, until at last it was heard. Once it was established that it was not some ghostly emanation making the racket, but in fact Tom, he was eventually extricated.

On a day's hunting there were usually three kindred spirits to be found on the heels of the hounds: the squire himself, Phoebe Higgs (one of his mistresses) and Tom Moody. Phoebe was as adventurous as the two men (or maybe more so). She and her horse would take on death-defying leaps, then smile sweetly at the squire from the other side, daring him to follow her. The squire had a clear field from the Clee Hills to the

Wrekin. Once they chased a fox to the top of the Wrekin and it fled through the Needle's Eye, leading the hounds behind it! They regularly went further still and hunted along the River Severn from source to sea. When there weren't enough hours in the day, they hunted by moonlight instead.

Tom stayed small, but strong. He always had a twinkle in his eye and was game for anything. His good humour made him a favourite of the hunt; he earned a good living from the squire and got plenty of tips on top, not to mention money from bets. It was rare that Tom would ever turn down a bet; no matter how crazy, he would find a way to do it. There were plenty of women who had a soft spot for Tom, but, like the squire, he never settled to just one woman and he never married.

It was a sad day when the squire gave up hunting, for none more than Tom. Tom was a good deal younger than the squire and he was a man born to hunt. His heart near broke as the shire's best steeds were sold off. Tom was kept on, together with his favourite foxhound, old Trojan, but Willey Hall was a different place.

Tom had always liked a drink and now he had a good deal more time on his hands. He spent more and more time down at the Hangster's Gate with his group of old cronies: Scale the schoolmaster, Crump the butcher and old Amen, the parson. The little inn was on the coach road between Bridgnorth and Wenlock. Tom's fame grew, and over time he became a tourist attraction, people asking to stop there to see him and hear his famous hunting cries. Tom helped put the inn on the map and the people who stopped always chalked up a few drinks on the board for him.

Tom used to boast that his 'constitution was as sound as a roach', but at the last he felt himself beginning to fail and asked to see his master.

'What is it, Tom?' asked the squire, and Tom replied:

My run is almost done and I'll be going to earth soon. When I am dead I wish to be buried at Barrow, under the yew tree, in the churchyard there. I wish to be carried to the grave by six earth stoppers. I wish for my horse, Old Soul, to follow me with my whip, boots, spurs, and cap, slung on the saddle and the brush of the last fox when I was up at the death at the side of his forelock. After my horse I want two couples of old hounds to follow me to the grave as mourners. When I am laid in the grave let three 'halloos' be given over me; and then, if I don't lift up my head, you may fairly conclude that Tom Moody is dead.

Tom died not long after, with the squire at his side, having managed to sip one last toast to the hunt and his old master.

All was done as he asked and three rattling 'halloos' sounded loud and clear over his grave. The crowd gathered and held their peace as the 'halloos' faded away and the grave stayed still and silent.

But though Tom was gone, he was not forgotten. The well-known songwriter Dibdin had stayed with Squire Forester and got to know Tom. When Tom died he wrote a song in memory of him. Charles Incledon, 'the human voice divine', was regularly filling Drury Lane Theatre and, when the song came out, he was one of the first to sing it. Squire Forester and some of his hunt made up a party to go to London to hear it. They took up their positions in the pit, sitting forward on their seats as the singer began the song. They were impressed enough with the verses, but his 'tally-ho' was sadly lacking. Charles Incledon was rather taken aback when the members of the Willey Hunt leapt up onto the stage and joined in the chorus to show how it should be done!

Back in Shropshire, though he did not rise from his grave on burial day, Tom didn't lie quiet; he couldn't bear to leave the hunt. On fine days, when the air was crisp, the hounds in full cry and the hunt sounding 'tally-ho', a fine melodious voice would sometimes mingle in with the call. At dawn, before the night was truly gone, Tom's shade would be seen in the early morning mist, fading with the sun.

Tom's ghost is rarely seen these days; he was a man of his time. The winds have changed and his days are gone. And yet, though the hunt rides to a different scent, when the baying of the hounds resounds across the land, sometimes an extra rider is seen following the hunt.

> Thus Tom spoke his friends, ere he gave us his breath,
> 'Since I see you're resolved to be in at the death,
> One favour bestow – 'tis the last I shall crave,
> Give a rattling view-hollow, thrice over my grave;
> And unless at that warning I lift up my head,
> My boys! You may fairly conclude I am dead!
> Honest Tom was obey'd and the shout rent the sky,
> For ev'ry voice join'd in the Tally-ho! cry,
> Tally-ho! Hark! forwards,
> Tally-ho! – Tally-ho!

The Fox's Knob

The main hunting season lasted from November to April, but before then, in the autumn, would be cub hunting. Cub hunting was used to train the young hounds to work as a pack, follow the horn and the calls of the huntsmen, and to get them used to the scent of a fox. It trained the foxes too – killing off the weaker cubs – teaching the ones who survived the call of the horn, the sound of the hounds and the importance of keeping their wits about them if they were to survive.

Hawkstone Park was the seat of the Hill family, and, as a family, they had a love of fox hunting and all that went with it. They always did their best to ensure a good day's hunting and a good night's feasting, which invariably led to, at some point, one of their guests lifting their glass and leading the toast, 'May the Hills of Shropshire last as long as the Shropshire Hills!'

All around Hawkstone was good hunting land, flat and open, with plenty of opportunities to flush the fox out from any cover, to flee ahead of the hounds, and give a breathless gallop to the field behind. Hawkstone itself was a good nursery for foxes, but terrible for hunting, with its rugged sandstone cliffs, narrow pathways, caves, bushes and brambles and a hundred opportunities for a fox to go to ground. A fox with the hounds on its scent would make for Hawkstone from miles around as a chance to escape the hunt.

There was one fox that had been born not far from Hawkstone. As a cub he had escaped the young hounds when the rest of his litter had not. Very quickly he learned to run fast and think faster. Each year he learned new tricks of evading the hounds: how to run up and down streams so that the hounds would lose his scent; jumping up and running along the tops of walls; squeezing through the thickest brambles and hedges to slow the horses behind the hounds, and always making sure he had new dens that the hunt had not found and couldn't earth up.

One year he found a tall tree that had fallen in the storms. The other trees had caught it, so that the trunk led almost up to the tree tops. He led the hounds to it, ran up the tree trunk, back over the hounds' and horses' heads, and leaped down behind the hunt, leaving them bewildered. Another time he stowed away in a farmer's cart and was given a ride far from the hunt.

The fox got a reputation with the hunt as 'Old Reynard', the wiliest fox around, and the entire hunt wanted to be present the day he was finally caught. The hunt would head to the place he had last been seen, trying to flush him out and finally outwit him.

As the seasons passed, Old Reynard was living up to his name. His fur was grizzling and the years were beginning to tell. He had sired many litters, but now his joints were stiffening and he was not as quick on his feet as he once had been. He knew he would not be able to outrun the hounds for ever.

As the winter came around he made a decision: the next time the hunt caught his scent he would lead them a last dance.

When the time came, he drew them across the fields and into the warren of Hawkstone. He was still quick and the horses thundered up the hillside behind the hounds. As they neared the top of the cliff, Reynard slowed, waving the white tip of his tail at the hounds. The baying crescendoed and the hounds lurched forward. Reynard made sure they were tightly in a pack close behind him, and then began his final flat out race for glory. With the hounds right on his heels, he sped to the summit, onto a stony outcrop jutting from the cliff, then launched over the edge with such speed that the hounds could not stop, their paws skittering and sliding. Their baying turned to whimpering as they plummeted down, down, down, following Reynard to his end.

Ever since, the red sandstone outcrop has been called Fox's Knob, in remembrance of Old Reynard.

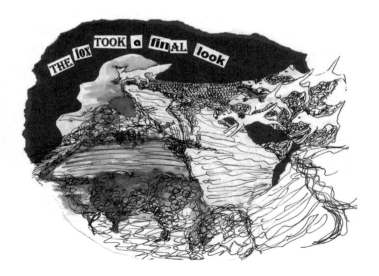

THE STOLEN CUP

Borders are magical places. The space where night meets day, water meets land, one world meets another. They are places where the walls between worlds are thin. All along the border where England meets Wales, there are wild places, untamed places full of mystery and otherness. Some are beautiful and alluring, others are threatening and disturbing.

Along the borders, nobles were of a slightly different breed to those who spent more time in court. The lords of the Marches were strong, rugged and rough mannered compared to the polished ways of court. They were warriors defending the border against the Welsh, but they were also men of the land. They understood that they lived on old land with ancient roots; that diplomacy was required, not just with their Welsh neighbours, but with the old ones, the fair ones, the ones who walked the forest long before mankind claimed the land.

In the eleventh century, Edric held land and estates throughout Shropshire and Herefordshire, but his stronghold was in South Shropshire. The care of his land and the people who lived on it was a matter of honour. He was known as a principled man, a great warrior and leader. He held out against William the Conqueror and cost him sorely in time, money and men.

Edric loved to hunt. One day, the ride had been fast and furious, and one by one his attendants had fallen away behind him until he was alone. He was deep in the forest when dusk fell. Although Edric thought he knew every inch of the forest, for once he was unsure where he was. As he stood, trying to catch his bearings, the sound of music drifted towards him. He followed the strains of music and they led him into a moonlit glade, where a group of women were dancing barefoot on the mossy grass. They were all extraordinarily beautiful, but the one in the centre took his breath away. In a trance, Edric ran amongst the women and wrapped his arms around her. The music stopped instantly and all the women turned on Edric.

He held fast to his prize and fought his way through the forest, maidens tearing at him tooth and nail like wildcats. He managed to reach his horse and carried the fairy woman away with him. He rode blindly through the trees, until they had left the women far behind, and came upon a path. Edric made his way to his nearest hall. The woman he had stolen sat herself by the fire and would not say a word. Edric tried to woo her with words and presents, but for three days and nights she sat silent and watching, never sleeping, never speaking. At last, at the end of the third day, she turned to Edric and said:

> I have watched you and how your people treat you these past three days. Your manners are rough, yet I've seen your little kindnesses and I've seen your brow crease as you search for the fairest outcome. I've seen that, above all, you are an honourable man. I have decided to stay with you and be your wife. But I am not like other women. I must be free to come and go as I please and you must not reproach me for my differences, nor where you found me, or my sisters in the wood. If you can agree to these terms, let us be wed – but be warned, if you break your word, I will be gone.

Edric listened to the lilt of her voice and smiled. His own stern countenance softened with love and he made his promise.

The two were married and rumours abounded about them. William the Conqueror heard the story of Edric's fairy bride and he invited them to a parley meeting. When he saw Godda, he smiled and said that such a radiant beauty could surely not be mortal. He did not want to deprive such a lovely woman of her husband, and so Edric and William made peace between them, though Edric never bent his knee to William (he was the only Saxon noble to neither submit nor be subdued). Edric and Godda were always welcome at court, but they were most content in Shropshire.

Further south along the border, Edric's cousin, the Earl of Hereford, had his seat at Sudeley, with lands and manors throughout Herefordshire. He was a man in the same mould as Edric and had the same knowledge of, and respect for, the land he held in trust. His family had held the land for generations and he had ridden and roamed through the Forest of Dean all his life; he knew its moods and seasons, its paths and pitfalls, like no other.

The Earl loved music and, like Edric, he loved to hunt. When he went out to hunt he always carried his flute with him. When the dogs caught the scent and the blood of the chase was up, he and his companions would thunder their mounts through the forest, the miles left behind with the dust from their hooves. But no matter how much land they covered, in the end they always came to Godfrey Hollow, in the Queen's Wood, to draw breath and rest a while.

Godfrey Hollow was a beautiful spot, a sheltered hollow, rimmed with trees. The grass was thick, mossy and soft to sit on. In the centre of the clearing was a little mound. The party would loosen their horses' girths and let them graze awhile while the men sat leaning against the mound. The Earl would bring out his flute and begin to play.

Whenever the glade filled with music, a young lad with bright eyes appeared on top of the mound, head cocked to one side listening, a drinking horn at his side. At the end of the tune, the Earl of Hereford would look up, his eyes finding the lad's and their gaze locking for a moment, before the lad held up his horn and presented it to the Earl. The Earl always took the first draught, bowed to the lad and passed the horn back. The boy offered the horn to each member of the hunt in turn. Everyone would take a drink and each would find liquid to their taste: ale, porter, wine or mead. No matter how many were on the hunt and how long a pull they took at the horn, there was always enough for all. When everyone had drunk and the horses were refreshed, the last to drink handed the horn back to the lad. They would bow their heads to him and then ride on.

It happened one time that a knight from the North was visiting. He joined the hunt and they had a hard morning's riding. It was

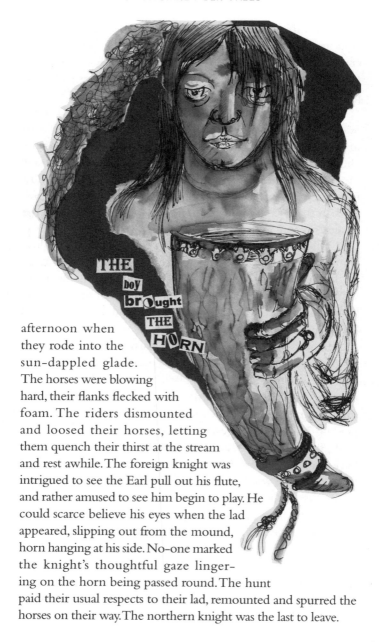

THE boy brought THE HORN

afternoon when
they rode into the
sun-dapphed glade.
The horses were blowing
hard, their flanks flecked with
foam. The riders dismounted
and loosed their horses, letting
them quench their thirst at the stream
and rest awhile. The foreign knight was
intrigued to see the Earl pull out his flute,
and rather amused to see him begin to play. He
could scarce believe his eyes when the lad
appeared, slipping out from the mound,
horn hanging at his side. No-one marked
the knight's thoughtful gaze lingering on the horn being passed round. The hunt
paid their usual respects to their lad, remounted and spurred the
horses on their way. The northern knight was the last to leave.

It was much later in the day that they halted again to rest.
With triumph, the northern knight pulled the drinking
horn from his saddle bag, calling them all to gather around
for another long draught of nectar.

The men looked at him with horror.

'What have you done?!' exploded the Earl, snatching the
horn away from the knight. 'Back, back, let us see if we can
put right the stupidity of this man! And you,' he hissed, turning back to the knight, 'You will pay dearly for this day's work.
To think that a man welcomed on my land would so destroy
my honour!'

They had ridden hard that day already, but it was nothing compared to the breakneck pace back to the hollow.
Dusk gathered around them, but the Earl knew every track
and path in that forest, and led them sure footed back to the
hollow.

The sun was only a memory when they returned and the
hollow was full of shadows. The Earl brought out his flute and
began to play. The music carried through the hollow, hanging
heavy in the night quiet. The glade was empty; no mischievous laughter, no twinkling eyes, no sign of the lad. The Earl
kept playing while the horses fidgeted, but the lad did not
come. At last he took the flute from his lips. The silence was
oppressive. They left the hollow without speaking. A man rode
on either side of the northern knight and he realised he was
under guard.

The solemn party headed back towards the Earl's castle
at Sudeley. As they made their way through Pershore, they
stopped at the bridge. The Earl faced the knight from the
north:

> You have sullied the name of knight. You have stolen from a most
> gracious host. You have dishonoured my name and I am not sure if
> I can right this wrong. You must pay with your life for your crime,
> though it will be but a drop in the ocean of debt you have caused.

They hanged the northern knight from the bridge. When his feet stopped kicking, the Earl himself cut the rope and watched the Avon take the body and carry it away to the sea. He did not merit a Christian burial.

Back at Sudeley, the Earl sat by the fire deep in thought. At last he summoned his men around him and spoke:

> We must return this horn to its rightful owner and I shudder to think what will happen if we fail. Our meetings at Godfrey Hollow were confirmation of an ongoing friendship, an acceptance of our presence in the wood, a permission of our hunting. Now the gates are closed to us at Godfrey Hollow, we must find another way to talk to the people of the wood and hope that they accept our apology. The only way I can think of is for us to visit my cousin, Edric, and to ask his wife Godda.

So the Earl of Hereford and a band of his men made their way north to Edric's lands, to find him in Clun Forest.

Edric's men saw the Hereford band approaching and Edric rode out to meet his cousin. One look at his cousin's face had Edric cancel the banquet and celebration that had begun preparation. Edric brought them back to his manor and called for Godda. As the story unfolded, Godda's face grew pale with fury, her lips tightening and her eyes glittering dangerously. The tale came to an end and the room filled with a heavy silence. The drinking horn sat accusingly on the table between them.

'We are sorry, Lady Godda, and we wish to return the horn to its rightful owner,' said the Earl.

'I must speak with my brother,' Godda replied, spitting out the words. Edric, the Earl and their men saddled their horses and Godda led them away from the hall, past the fields and through forest, until she led them up to a windswept hilltop and a circle of stones.

'Dismount from your horses and stay on the outside of the stones,' commanded Godda as she strode into the centre of the circle. She spoke to the breeze, her voice strange and melodious. They saw shadows gathering within the circle, indistinct at first, slowly taking on form and weight, until a group of men stood around Godda listening to her.

The Earl stood watching at Edric's side. He saw the bearing of the men, how they were dressed, and rapidly realised that his audience with Godda's brother was with the King himself. He watched as Godda passed on the story; he saw the building tension and anger, the fierce glances in his direction. At last, the King and his followers turned and stood facing the Earl of Hereford at Edric's side. The Earl stood tall, accepting the waves of anger washing towards him.

'I am sorry,' he said. 'I wish I could change what has happened, but I cannot. What was done, was done without sanction and the offender has been put to death. We wish to return the horn to its rightful owner.' He held the horn out towards the circle.

Godda's brother, King of the Fair Folk, stepped forwards, shaking his head. 'We cannot take back the horn. Its rightful owner perished when the horn was taken. The horn is now your responsibility. Your honour depends upon its safety.'

The men within the circle were becoming less distinct, fading back into the mist. Godda stepped between the stones, mounted her horse and, without a word, galloped back towards Edric's manor.

The others followed more slowly. Edric asked his cousin to stay and visit for a while, but the Earl smiled sadly and shook his head, all too aware of the frosty atmosphere emanating from Godda. He and his men travelled home and the horn weighed heavy at his side.

The Earl of Hereford did keep the horn safe during his lifetime. Later, in troubled times, one of his descendents placed the horn in the Palace of Westminster, for safe-keeping, and there it stayed until the days of Oliver Cromwell. From then, the trail goes cold. Perhaps the horn perished when the palace burnt down. Perhaps it was moved to a museum storeroom and sits gathering dust, its significance forgotten. Or perhaps it finally made its way home to another guardian.

THE HOUND ON THE HILL

The Long Mynd is a ten-mile ridge stretching out to the south of Church Stretton, a long brown wall on the horizon. It is a steep climb to the rugged moorland on top; a land of heather and whinberry, rush and grass. On a clear day the top of the Mynd is beautiful, with views across Shropshire, Herefordshire, Wales and Cheshire. But even on a summer's day it is a wild and remote place; buzzards circle upwards on the Mynd's thermals, their plaintive cry a common sound. The land is deceptive; bog and marsh masquerading as firm grass-land. The flat-looking upland plateau creases into a myriad of little valleys, known as batches and hollows. In winter it draws the snow and even a thin blanket is treacherous, disguising the tracks and their markers, lying lightly over hidden hollows and making the descent a terrifying battle against gravity. Its serene beauty is undermined by place names such as Devil's Mouth and Deadman's Hollow; even the December fair at Church Stretton became known as Deadman's Fair. Each year drunken revellers would stagger homeward after sunset, their unsteady steps wending across the Long Mynd. Every year there were some who never made it home.

It is not just the landscape, weather and loneliness that makes the Long Mynd a daunting place to travel at night, but the spirits and shades that shelter there. Up between the Portway and Ratlinghope is a hollow where 'there is always something to be seen'; a funeral procession making its way along the road, a hearse creaking and rattling by, the road thick with mourners behind it. Wild Edric sometimes roams the slopes in the form of a great black dog with fiery eyes. At other times, his Wild Hunt whirls over the Long Mynd and across South Shropshire, the blast of Edric's horn heralding

disaster, disease or death to come. The hunt comes with a tre-
mendous rushing wind. The thundering hooves mingle with
the baying hounds, producing an overwhelming noise that
pounds in every vein and fibre.

One evening, a young lad was making his way home over
the Long Mynd, his errands done. It had been a beautiful day,
but now the sun was low in the sky and the shadows were
lengthening. He walked briskly. He knew the track well, but
he also knew the stories, and he had a healthy respect for the
road; he would prefer to get home before dark if he could.
A movement in the heather caught his eye. Looking closer he
saw a patch of white and red, and then heard a whine.

'Hey, boy,' he said softly, 'what are you doing up here on
your own? C'mon, let's have a look at you and get you back
home.' With that flash of white and red fur, he assumed it
must be a young foxhound, footsore and separated from the
pack. He picked a handful of leaves and dipped them in a
pool of water.

'Here boy, let's bind up those paws for you and get you to
the kennels.'

The dog came out from the heather. It was no foxhound.
It must have been lying in a dip, for it was the size of a calf,
with a rough white coat and red ears. The boy's hands holding
the leaves began to shake. It was a 'Hound of the Hill', a fairy
hound, one of the Wild Hunt's hounds. Still, it was too late
now; he'd talked to it already and here it was, looking at him
and waiting. He couldn't walk on and pretend not to see it
now. So he mustered his courage, gently lifted the paws one by
one and bound up the pads.

He tipped his cap to the dog and said, 'There you go, Sir,
now your paws will get you back to your home and I'll be
off to mine.' The Hound wagged its tail and disappeared off
into the heather. The lad pulled his jacket close about him and
walked briskly back home.

The seasons turned; nothing bad happened and the lad
stopped thinking about his encounter. But one evening the

THE boy bandaged the paw

lad was making his way home along the same road. This time
night had fallen; the track was slick with rain and the drizzle
sucked the heat out of him. The road led up and down the
hollows of the summit and, as the lad climbed out of a dip, he
saw ahead of him a huge black beast, an enormous dog with
eyes like fire. The lad froze. It was Edric: Edric at his most wild;
his humanity forgotten; a creature of loss, rage and vengeance;
the instinct to hunt and kill pounding in its ears. It lifted its
great head to smell the air and then turned toward the lad, its
eyes settling on him like two glowing coals. The boy knew
that he mustn't run or speak, but it took all his strength to
stand firm as the hound padded towards him with slow, delib-
erate steps.

The breath grew ragged in the boy's chest. The fiery eyes
drew level with his own. He braced himself for whatever
might come; then something white and red exploded from
the undergrowth and barrelled into the black dog. Taken by
surprise, the black dog was knocked to the ground, but in a
moment it was up. The lad saw the great white and red Hound
of the Hill take stance opposite the black apparition, and for a
moment the two circled each other. Then both leapt forward

and the two dogs fought, snarling and growling, worrying at each other, biting, tearing, tumbling over one another. The lad stood rooted to the ground, watching. The terrible noise of the battle rent the night. At last the two dogs split apart to prowl in a circle around one another. The black dog stood still for a moment, staring at the red and white hound, and then moved its glowing eyes to rest on the lad. Suddenly it turned and loped off into the darkness.

The panting hound looked at the lad, his tongue hanging out of his mouth. His tail gave a wag, but the lad knew better than to thank the animal. Slowly the boy put his hand to his cap and nodded his head.

'Good night, Sir.'

The Hound vanished into the night and the lad walked safely home.

Six

WATERY WOMEN AND A WOODLAND MAIDEN

THE ASRAI

> A riddle, a riddle, what can it be?
> A riddle, a riddle, can you tell me?
> I tremble at each breath of air
> And yet can the heaviest burdens bear

The smallest pebble splashes through the surface, tumbling down towards the depths, and yet such great weights can sit on top of the water, never knowing what lies beneath. They never know what the water supports, what creatures live within its realm. Even today, explorers never know for sure what lies just beyond the reach of their fingertips, just beyond where sight will take them.

Tom was out on the mere in Ellesmere. He was out in his boat on a short summer night. It had been hot and the air was still warm. In the houses, the windows were open and blankets lay discarded. On the mere, the air was cooler and there was just the hint of a breeze whispering in the reeds, rippling the water and gently rocking the boat.

Tom's nets were set and he had nothing to do but wait for the fish to swim into them. He lay back in the boat, enjoying the quiet stillness of the night. The cool breeze caressed his cheek, and the branches overhanging the mere were silhouetted black against the velvet night sky. The moon was rising now, a full moon, fat and heavy, slowly clambering upwards, above the branches and into the sky to join the stars. Tom's eyelids drooped, fluttering open every so often to see the moon a little higher, then closing again.

At last the moon began to sink. Tom knew that soon he would have to move, haul up his nets, row to the far side of the mere, and hide his boat under the brambles for another day.

He stretched out, uncurling his fingers and toes, and sat up with a yawn. He took hold of the net and began to pull. The net was heavy and Tom, wide awake now, smiled and began to pull harder in anticipation of the full load of gleaming fish. He gave one last heave and hauled the net over the side and into the boat. But it wasn't the slippery silvery bundle he had expected. He stared. He saw pale white limbs, thick shining tresses, two arms fastened tight around two knees and two big eyes staring up at him. Tom's mouth fell open in disbelief. Then he began to remember the stories – stories told by the fire in the pub – stories he had scoffed at. He remembered the tales of a race of people living beneath the mere, who only came up once in a hundred years to bathe in the light of the full moon and to grow. A people called the Asrai.

There was a whimper from the bottom of the boat and then the Asrai began to speak. Her voice was like rain on the reeds, a whisper on the water. Tom didn't understand a word, but he heard the longing, the need of a salmon fighting its way home. Without thinking he bent down and began to unfasten the knots binding her. But then he did begin to think. He thought about his children and how they all needed new shoes. He thought about this Asrai in his nets and how he now had no fish to sell or eat. He thought of how much the people up at the big house would pay to have an Asrai swimming in their fishponds. All these thoughts flashed through his mind; he hardened his heart and tightened the knots. He pulled out the oars and rowed toward the far side of the mere.

The song of the Asrai got louder and one arm pushed its way through the net, pointing towards the sinking moon and the brightening eastern sky. She caught hold of Tom's arm to get his attention, but the moment she touched him, she snatched her hand away as though burnt. And Tom, he could still feel the imprint of her fingers, a cold band of moonlight wrapped around his elbow.

Tom let his oars rest and reached over the side of the boat, pulling up armfuls of reeds. He spread them over the Asrai to keep her skin moist, but also to hide the fear and confusion in the eyes staring up at him.

Tom rowed hard, putting his back into the oars, making his way across the water to the overhanging bushes where he kept

his boat. He splashed out of the boat and into the shallows, pulling his boat up onto the bank. He reached down to lift the the reeds out of the way, to gather up the Asrai and take her home. But as he bent down, the sun rose over the trees and the first fingers of sunlight reached into the boat. Beneath the reeds nothing was left but a puddle of mere water.

Tom stood silent and wistful in the dawn. At last he slowly turned and walked home. There was nothing to show for his night's work, nothing but a cold ache in his elbow, and in his heart a colder ache still.

MORWEN OF THE WOODLANDS

It was in the days when Prince Benlli was the prince of Powys. He was a true prince of his time: he defended and extended the borders of Powys; he was a strong leader, but a fair one; he was a man of action. He loved the song of battle and the thrill of the chase, but, when at home in his hall, he liked nothing better than to go to the hunt.

One day Benlli was out hunting. He started a white hart. Benlli, single-minded, pursued that hart, not noticing the other hunters fall away behind him. There was nothing in the world for him except that hart, his own heart beating in time with his horse's hooves as they pounded their way through the forest. The hart twisted and turned, leaping over fallen trees, diving under low branches, but still Benlli was hard on its heels.

Deep, deep, deep into the forest they went, until something flickered at the corner of Benlli's eye. He turned his head; there was nothing there. Again, there was something white amongst the shadows of the branches. The leaves around him seemed to jangle his name. He looked forward; the hart was gone. He looked back and realised his retinue had been out-paced, he was alone. Once more the flicker caught his eye and as he turned, he saw that the white flicker was a dress.

Inside that dress was the most beautiful woman he had ever seen. Her hair flowed thick and silky; it made his hands long to reach out and touch it. His eyes locked with hers, and the forest, his land, his life, everything, fell away until she was the only thing in the world. He slid from his horse, his arms outstretched towards her to pull this vision closer, but his arms closed around nothing. She was gone and the light had fled from the forest.

He stood there, beguiled by her, a wistful smile at the memory of his encounter on his face. So it was that his friends and followers found him. Their clamour and familiar voices woke him from his reverie and they made their way back, empty-handed, to Benlli's hall.

As soon as Benlli slipped into sleep that night, she came to him again. Her face shimmered just before him, but every time he reached out she slipped between his fingers. He woke in the grey half-light of dawn, stole down to the stables, saddled his horse and was away.

Throughout the day he searched the forest. His eyes hunted from root to trunk, trunk to branch and branch to leaf, restlessly roaming the twilight beneath the trees for a glimpse of a white dress, the light falling on her silken hair.

Then ahead of him there was a white flicker. Benlli's eyes brightened and he urged his horse on. But no matter how hard he spurred his horse, or how fast they travelled, the flicker was always just ahead, tantalizingly close, until at last he cried out, 'My lady, will you not wait!?'

She stopped and his horse slid to a halt. 'All you had to do, my lord, was ask.' Her voice was like a cool breeze on a hot summer's day.

'Who…who…are…you?' asked Benlli in wonder.

'You may call me Morwen of the Woodlands,' she replied.

'Morwen,' he repeated. Benlli tasted the name and found that it fitted well. 'Morwen, since I saw you yesterday, I have been able to think of nothing else. You have stolen my heart. Please, give me your hand in exchange.'

Morwen eyed him up and down. 'But Benlli, you already have a wife!'

The colour rose in Benlli's cheeks and he returned, 'Yes, it's true. But it is many years since we wed. All is not well between us. I did love her once, but…now…now I have seen you and I could never love her as I love you!'

Morwen looked at Benlli long and hard, until at last she spoke:

Very well. I will be your bride. But there are conditions. You must put your first wife away. And secondly, you must realise, Benlli, I am no mortal woman. I am one of the *Twyleth Teg*, the Fair Folk, and although I will live with you, I must return to my people for one whole day each week, from sunrise to sunrise, and you must never question me or try to follow me. If you will promise me this, I will be your wife.

Benlli gladly consented. He swept her up into his arms, gently lifted her onto the horse and took his new bride home.

When they arrived home, Benlli called for his first wife, but, though they searched high and low, she was nowhere to be found. Benlli assumed she had already heard the tidings and he put her out of his head; his every thought was saved for Morwen.

The wedding was held that very day in haste and joy. Benlli and Morwen made the perfect couple. People commented on how well they were suited and how it seemed as though they had known each other for years. Morwen knew Benlli's every mood; when he needed to laugh, when he needed quiet, when he wanted her by his side and when he needed to be alone – though it was rare he did not wish Morwen to be with him.

In those first few months the only time Benlli was unhappy was the day each week when Morwen was gone. The hours dragged by until she returned home. Those long hours gave Benlli time to brood and he began to wonder why she had to go back every week, why once a fortnight or month would not suffice. Why did she need to go back so often? Didn't she love him the way he loved her? Did she not feel the same torment at being parted? Why did she never ask him to go with her? He wanted to show her off to the world and yet he had never met any of her kin.

So the seeds of doubt were planted. Slowly they grew into worms that burrowed into the dark places of his soul. They gnawed away at him until he was so full of distrust and anger that he could barely look Morwen in the eye when she was home. Benlli took himself away from his hall and away from Morwen. He took out his frustration on the neighbouring Princedoms, pushing back the borders and winning more land for Powys.

After one such campaign, the prince and his soldiers had won a large piece of land to the south and returned to Benlli's hall to celebrate. The hall was full of people, rich and poor alike, for the poor had fought shoulder to shoulder with the rich. All Benlli's men were there, with their women at their side, but Benlli stood alone. When he had arrived home, Morwen was nowhere to be found – she was in the woods and would not return until the next morning. Benlli sat with his men, drinking and laughing with unsmiling eyes.

There was another man at the table who did not have a woman by his side. His name was Wylan and he was a monk, an honoured guest. Unbeknown to Benlli and his abbey, his heart had been seduced by greed and envy and he had become a sorcerer.

Wylan kept his eyes fixed on Benlli throughout the banquet. When the meal had been eaten, the guests carried on drinking, the men describing in detail the exploits of their latest win. Wylan made his way over to Benlli and, taking his arm, guided him to a dark corner of the hall.

'Your Highness, I see the clouds in your eyes; you have deep troubles. Will you not share them with me?'

Benlli looked into Wylan's dark eyes. For the first time his lips unsealed and all his troubles came out; his fears and fantasies about Morwen, how she lived within his grasp and yet he could not seem to hold her.

Wylan listened to all Benlli had to say. He replied:

> I can give you peace of mind, my prince. But peace of mind is
> the greatest gift that man can receive and as such it carries a high
> price. I can give you peace of mind, but in return you must prom-
> ise the monks of the abbey a fee, and you must give me Morwen.

Benlli heard the promise, but not the price. He agreed. Wylan
hurried out of the hall before the mead lost its effect and
Benlli could change his mind.

Deeper and deeper into the woods he hastened, until, at nearly
midnight, he came to the heart of the woods. He sat down in the
undergrowth next to a heap of rocks and began to chant:

> May Prince Benlli be at peace
> May Prince Benlli have peace of mind
> For he has promised the monks a gift
> And myself also
> For I shall have Morwen of the woodlands
> She must come to me at dawn at the abbey
> There I will meet her and greet her
> And make her my wife.

On and on Wylan chanted through the night, until at last there
was a glimmer of grey in the east and the night was nearly
over. Wylan rose to his feet and made his way towards the
abbey.

He reached the abbey in the half-light of near dawn, but
something was there before him. Huddled on the steps of the
abbey was a dark shape. It lifted its head and Wylan saw the ugli-
est face he had ever seen. Greasy, straggly hair hung limp around
a mass of warts and dirt lines, and in the centre two bright, black
darting eyes. Wylan slowly edged a little closer and he could
make out long gangly limbs beneath the shapeless shift.

'Wylan,' a dry cracked voice called to him, 'Wylan, come sit
and wait with me.'

Wylan slowly made his way to the steps and sat at the other end from the hag. The sour smell of unwashed skin and musty clothes attacked his nostrils.

'Good morning, Wylan. I know why you're here and it is not yet quite dawn. Let me tell you a story while we wait. Once, long ago, I was young and beautiful.'

Wylan snickered, but she continued:

I was so beautiful that they called me the 'Flower of Powys'. At that time the prince, Benlli, was also young and looking for a bride. It was only natural that I should be given to him. For a while we were happy. I fell in love with that young man; I loved him truly, and in his own way he loved me too. But as the years went by I lost my beauty and, with it, I lost Benlli's love. In desperation, like you, I turned to sorcery and magic. I turned to the Fair Folk, the *Twyleth Teg*. I made a bargain with them that for six days of the week I would be young and beautiful once more, but for the seventh day I should remain with them in the shape of a hag. And so with my newfound beauty I went once more to my lord, and again I won his heart. We have lived in contentment since then; but last night someone chanted an evil spell, pulling me from the Fair Folk before my day was spent, and now I am doomed to remain as a hag for the rest of my life!

But come, Wylan, the sun is peeping over the hills – its light touches our toes. It is time for us to be wed.

Wylan jumped up, his eyes wide and panicked. He backed away to the door of the abbey. His hands firm against the wood, he cried, 'May Prince Benlli have peace. May you, Morwen, have peace. May I myself have peace and God forgive me!' He pushed the door open, threw himself inside and slammed the door behind him. From that time on he turned his back on sorcery and lived as a good monk should!

Later that day Benlli was sat beside the fish pools. His head was still fuzzy but, with a turning stomach, he remembered more clearly what he had agreed with Wylan. He sat with his head in his hands – remorse, anger and loss battling for control. Suddenly, something made him look up and he turned and stared towards the woods. There, walking towards him, was a woman. He gazed at her. In that woman he saw his old wife and new wife in one. He leapt to his feet and ran towards her. They held onto each other long and tight, and by the time they let go, peace had been made between them.

From that time on Benlli and his wife were side by side each and every day of the week, and they grew old together. Now when Benlli looked at his wife, he didn't see the lines around her eyes, but the smiles that had made them. When he took her hand in his, he did not notice how time had gnarled her fingers, but felt the strength she gave him.

When their time came to them, as it must to all men and women, they were given the greatest blessing of all; for Benlli and his wife died in their bed on the same night. And with their death came a sigh. There was a sound of grating rock, a rumble of moving earth and slowly the hall began to sink. Deeper and deeper into the earth it sank, then soft rain began to fall and covered the hall with water.

The lake is still there – Llynclys Pool. It is tucked away, encircled by trees. But if you have the will, you can make your

THE castle sank into the lake

way down the old railway track and gaze on the still waters, and sometimes you may catch a glimpse of the hall below. The pool is named for the hall drowned in its depths: *Llynclys*, the swallowed court.

MRS ELLIS

Age is a strange thing. It distils personality into its essential essence. While some people mellow, maturing in wisdom, knowledge and patience, others become sour and resentful. Mrs Ellis was one of the latter. Her husband died young, before they had children, and she lived alone in a little cottage, brewing up bitterness.

The one joy Mrs Ellis treasured was her well. It was fed by a spring and she guarded it jealously. The water from that well was pure, crystal clear and sweet to drink. The problem was that everyone else knew about the spring and people were always coming to her house and begging some of the water; they wouldn't leave her alone. People said that the water was medicinal; it would cure sore eyes and aid the digestion. Mrs Ellis wouldn't give it away, but she did sell it – in tiny, high priced bottles.

One year there was a drought. The rivers shrank from their banks and many of the springs dried up. Mrs Ellis' spring seemed to grow stronger. Every day flocks of people would come and ask for water. Mrs Ellis offered to sell it, but the people couldn't afford her prices. Instead they crept back at night, trampling over her land and sending clouds of dust into the air. Lying in bed, Mrs Ellis could hear the chain rattling up and down, pulling bucket after bucket of water. She was fuming. They came back one night to find that there was a lid over the well with a lock. The people had to leave thirsty, their throats parched, and search for water elsewhere.

Under the ground, the spring kept bubbling, feeding water into the well. There was no one to take away any of the water. It bubbled higher and higher, until it reached the lid that was chained down over the top of the well. The wooden lid was enough to keep people from the water, but it couldn't keep the water from the people. The water lifted the lid, tightening the chains. It trickled over the top and down the sides of the well, slowly at first, and then as the force grew greater, the lid began to rattle. The chains strained as the water poured through the gaps and the pressure built beneath the lid. At last a chain-link snapped and the water erupted upwards, sending the lid flying into the sky.

In the morning, the people looked out of their windows to discover a brand new lake sparkling and glimmering under the sun. They ran down with their buckets and bowls and drank their fill. There was no sign of Mrs Ellis, her cottage or the well. They named the mere after the woman whose selfishness had created it, 'Mrs Ellis' Mere', Ellesmere. They never did find Mrs Ellis. But some have seen her since. She still lives in the mere, prowling around the edges, trying to keep the water for herself. The long years in the water have made her hair long and tangled, straggly like pondweed. Her nails have grown long, sharp and twisted. Her teeth are green with pond algae. She waits close to the water's edge, just below the surface, ready to pounce and drag any strangers down, down, down, never to surface again.

There have been a few, children mostly, who managed to tear themselves free from her clutches and run screaming back home. Not knowing the story of Mrs Ellis, they told of long straggly hair and green hungry teeth, and gave her the name Jenny Greenteeth. Even today, children are warned not to go too close to the water's edge for fear of Jenny Greenteeth.

Seven

STRANGE HAUNTINGS

THE WHITE LADY OF OTELEY

Above Ellesmere, with beautiful landscaped gardens overlook-
ing the water, stands the new Oteley Hall. All that is left of the
old hall is a chimney, the worn brickwork surrounded by long
grass. It is the haunt of the White Lady of Oteley.

Down below, the White Lady's Causeway leads into the
mere. In the early 1800s, swimmers used to follow it into the
water until the water grew too deep. It was forgotten until
1879, when divers rediscovered it during their search for the
body of a drowned man. The last attempt that I know of to
follow it down into the depths was during the Second World
War. Two airmen, stationed nearby, were having a drink
with some of the locals. Talk turned to the mere, its stories
and the causeway beneath the water. As the beer flowed, the
airmen laughed and vowed to investigate the next day. Bound
to their word, the next afternoon, with a small group gathered to watch, the two men stripped off and waded into the
water. They found the causeway and followed it into the mere,
laughing and joking, while their spectators heckled them

good-naturedly. The two men ducked their heads under the water to swim a bit deeper and see how far they could follow the causeway. Their audience waited for them to come back up and report on what they'd seen. The seconds ticked by; the chat and laughter petered into silence. The surface of the mere was calm. The two airmen never resurfaced and their bodies were never found; they simply vanished into the mere.

The daughter of Oteley Hall was young, educated and beautiful. She was of an age to be married and her father was negotiating a suitable match. The young woman had other ideas. Each day, looking out of her window, her eyes lingered on the stable yard, watching the young groom at work. Feeling her eyes upon him, he would turn to meet her gaze, a smile lighting his face, before dragging his eyes away and turning back to work. The two met in secret trysts, declaring their love. When the young lady's betrothal was announced, they made plans to elope. The groom was to wait at night in the boathouse and the girl would slip out of a window, once the household was asleep, to meet him. Together they would row across to the other side of the mere, where the groom had arranged for two horses to be waiting. By morning they would be far away.

But the girl's father overheard their plans. Silently fuming, he let the day run its course. His daughter retired to her room early, claiming a headache. With his gun under his arm he went to meet her lover.

The groom was waiting. He jumped to his feet in welcome as someone entered the boathouse, expecting his sweetheart. The gun fired and the lad fell back, dead, into the boat. The father rowed out over the water and rolled the weighted body into the mere. His work done, he returned to the house to let the evening play out and his daughter find she had been jilted.

Up at the house, only pretending to sleep, the girl heard the shot and her heart grew cold. She slipped out of the window and ran across the lawns. She watched as her father heaved something out of the boat to splash into the mere. She hid in the trees while her father rowed back and tied up the boat. She watched him leave the boathouse, dread gripping her heart as she saw the dark shadow of the gun under his arm. As he walked back across the gardens, she flew into the boat-house. There was a dark smear in the shadows at the bottom of the boat. She dipped her fingers in the viscous puddle and tasted the salt tang of blood. Grief racked her body. Salt tears mingled with the mere water as she waded out through the

A ghostly figure AT THE edges of the mere

rushes to join her love. Deeper and deeper she went, until the cold water closed over her head.

She did not rest easy. Soon after her death, a ghostly white figure was seen around the edges of the mere. The daughter haunted Oteley Hall and the lawns that led to the water, and accidents began to happen more and more frequently in the hall. Each time the food was spoiled, or a piece of china crashed to the floor, the maids would look fearfully around for the White Lady. It became more and more difficult to find staff that would stay at the hall.

Eventually, in the early 1900s, the old Oteley Hall was demolished and the family moved to a new hall built in the same grounds. But when the old hall was knocked down, they left a chimney as a home for the White Lady, hoping she would not follow them into the new residence.

The Boogies and the Saltbox

There was once a farmer by the name of Reynalds. He was a wealthy man, with plenty of land and several properties to his name around the area. The time came for him to be married to another landowner's daughter.

The preparations were made, both for the wedding and afterwards. His bride to be had her eye on his house at Gorsty Bank. It was a grand place, though perhaps a little old-fashioned. No one remembered quite when it had been built; people said that the gentry had lived there once upon a time.

Well, Mr Reynalds had a nagging doubt somewhere at the back of his mind about that old house, but he could think of no good reason to say no, and he wanted to please his betrothed.

So he sent a team to check everything over, clean up, do all the repairs and air the old place. By the time the big day came, the house was gleaming and filled with flowers to welcome the newlyweds.

Of course, the new Mrs Reynalds wanted to put her stamp on the place, to give it a woman's touch. She scattered her linens throughout the house, smoothed her embroidered tablecloth over the table and, last of all, brought out a beautiful silver saltbox – a family heirloom – and put it in pride of place on the dresser.

'There. Now it feels like a proper home!' she declared.

But the honeymoon period was short. There was already a couple living at the farm. Two old, wizened faces peered down from the rafters like two apples, dried and crinkled after being stored for the winter. They sat unseen, watching all the preparations taking place. They smiled as the bridegroom carried his bride over the threshold. It had been a long and lonely time since they had enjoyed company.

At first it was little things, easily brushed off. Mrs Reynalds' mirror went missing from her dresser and was eventually found under her pillow, but not before she'd accused all the maids of taking it. The broom was never where the maids left it; the milk turned sour quicker than it did anywhere else, and the fox got in and killed the chickens.

The lads and maids began to whisper about there being bad luck about the farm, and trying to get a new place at the next fair. None of the maids liked being alone in the house; they would feel eyes watching them and would catch movements at the edge of their vision. The cowman, who would bring the cows in for milking in the half-light before dawn, talked of two shadows skulking along the hedgerow behind him.

When Mr Reynalds first heard the rumours he laughed them off. But he had a nagging disquiet and couldn't help but wonder why the place had lain empty for so long. Soon, he too saw the shadows; two dark figures and a quiet chuckle accompanied any mishap or bad fortune at the farm.

One day the youngest maid, Hannah, got locked in the root cellar and was trapped alone in the dark for hours before they found her. In floods of tears, she told anyone who would listen how she had sat huddled in a corner while laughter danced around her and unseen hands pulled her hair and pinched her black and blue. She packed her bags, left first thing the next morning, and never mind her fee.

Mr Reynalds, feeling rather foolish, decided to seek help. He made his way into town and went to see Tom, the black-smith, farrier and man of wisdom. Mr Reynalds waited for a quiet moment before dipping his head under the lintel. Tom looked up from the forge, his face lit by the glow.

'Ah. I wondered how long it would be before you came through that doorway. Give me an hour to finish my work and put the forge to bed, then we'll take a walk,' Tom said.

The two set off across the fields and climbed up towards the Callow. They sat looking down over the farm and Tom imparted his advice:

> The problem is that on your farm you have a couple of boogies. No, no, they're not ghosts, they were never human. No one knows quite where they come from, and it's probably best not to talk about it too loud or for too long. But they are old spirits, without souls, without consciences. They have made a home in that old place and they've taken to you and your family. As I see it, you have three possible choices: you can either learn to live with them, you can banish them, or you can move out.

Mr Reynalds opened his mouth to speak, but Tom held up his hand and carried on::

> Those are your options, but it may not be that easy. Your ances-tors ended up moving out and I doubt that was their first choice. There are lots of things you can try, but I don't hold out much hope that they'll work. Those spirits have lived apart from humans for a long while, and they're having fun, but you may be able to tame them. Be polite; be neighbourly. Tip your hat and say 'Good evening' if you feel they're near. Try leaving a bowl of cream out for them. If you can get them to help you instead of torment you, they'll be the best thing that ever happened to that farm.

Mr Reynalds went home and told his wife what Tom had said. They gathered their staff together and told them to be polite to the 'neighbours', and their plan of leaving cream out each night.

But the attempt did not work. Their gestures of friendship were received with snickers of laughter and raspberry blowing. The cream was not drunk, but instead left as a trail of milky footprints through the house, whipped and daubed over the windows and used to drown the cat.

The spirits were becoming bolder and more clearly defined. All who lived at the farm regularly saw glimpses of the old man or old woman here or there, usually followed by some sort of mischief. At night, when the household had gone to bed, they would creep in like cats and curl up by the fire.

Only a few days after his first visit, Mr Reynalds was back on Tom's doorstep.

'I think those boogies have got too strong a hold on that place now, but try and banish them if you will. I'll write you some charms to hide through the house and I think you should get the minister in,' Tom said.

The boogies slept by the fire

Mr Reynalds went and talked to the minister. The next day, Mr Reynalds hid the charms, one in each room and barn. The minister arrived with his book under his arm, lit his candle and began to read. The room filled with laughter, a shadowy form appeared next to the minister and the old woman blew out the candle. From the rafters, the old man tipped over a jug of cream, covering the minister and soaking the pages of the bible. While the minister nobly tried to continue from memory, the pair tormented him by pinching and prodding, pushing and shoving. The minister batted at them like flies, but they crowded round him like smoke. He could neither touch nor escape them, until he pushed his way out of the farm and fled down the road, swearing never to set foot in the damned place again.

'I thought it would probably come to this,' said Tom, as he sat on the grass with Mr Reynalds after the incident. 'Those spirits have deep roots in that old farm. If you really want rid of them, it will take some doing. You need to leave, but be discreet.'

Surreptitiously the Reynalds' started moving things out and sending them to a smaller farm that they owned. At last, the day of leaving arrived. The two spirits were curled up in front of the fire as the couple silently gathered their last few belongings and loaded them onto a cart. The horses' feet had been muffled and they quietly left the farm to start afresh.

Reynalds and his wife set to work at making their home in the new farm, unpacking all their belongings. It soon transpired that somehow, Mrs Reynalds' saltbox had been left behind. She was in a terrible state and was determined that it must be retrieved immediately. Well, of course, Mr Reynalds wouldn't let his wife go back; instead he sent the cowman to go and fetch it, telling him he must not be seen. The cowman was not pleased with the job, but he agreed and set off with young Edward, the stable lad, to keep him company.

The two dawdled down the road, and they hadn't gone far when they saw the old woman and the old man walking towards them. There was nothing shadowy about them; bold as brass they came stepping along the way, their two old faces crinkling into smiles when they saw the cowman and Edward. The boogies danced up to the visitors, brandishing before them the forgotten silverware. 'We've brought your saltbox!' they announced.

There was nothing for it but to turn around, and the four of them walked to the new farm together.

Mrs Reynalds saw them coming first and her face turned ashen. One of the maids ran squeaking into the house and a moment later, Mr Reynalds came out and stood with his arm around his wife's waist. He gave her a squeeze and they both smiled at the couple and pretended to be delighted to see them. It was a cold day. With a meaningful look, they told the cowman to make sure the fire was going well in the kitchen, and to tell the cook to set some food to welcome their guests. While all was being got ready, the Reynalds' showed the old couple around the new farm.

When they went into the kitchen, a great fire was blazing. Beef and beer were set ready on the table. In front of the fire a thick, fresh bed of straw had been strewn to make a comfortable place for the boogies to sit. Underneath the straw, unmoving and unseen, Tom lay hidden, waiting. The boogies sat down with the Reynalds' and ate and talked. When their bellies were full, the boogies couldn't resist the fire any more and made their way to sit on the straw and warm themselves by the flames.

That was the moment Tom had been waiting for. From beneath the straw, he leapt up and tumbled the two spirits into the fire, straw and all. Then Tom and Farmer Reynalds grabbed hold of the pitchforks and brooms waiting ready, and beat the two back, keeping them on the fire until they shrivelled to nothing but dust and ashes. Tom and Mr Reynalds put down their implements and, together with Mrs Reynalds and the farm staff, they silently watched the fire burn down.

That was the end of the two boogies, with their meddling and mischief. The Reynalds' went back to Gorsty Bank and spirits never troubled the place again.

THE ROARING BULL OF BAGBURY

There was once a farmer who lived at Bagbury Farm in
Hyssington. He had a reasonable farm, but he was mean.
He had to travel round all the hiring fairs in Shropshire and
Montgomeryshire to find enough workers, for none who
knew of him would be foolish enough to work for him. Those
that did soon discovered their mistake. Many did not last out
their agreed six months, and those that did never stayed any
longer. He would order the thinnest gruel and oldest lefto-
vers to be set before the workers, while he himself would
always eat of the best. The bothy was draughty and cold, but
he would not hear of them taking the animals' straw to make
beds; they had to make do with the cold floor. If he caught
any worker stealing food, bedding or clothes, they would be
flogged in the yard.

His animals fared little better; they were thin and overworked. He was a cruel man, quick with his tongue and the
whip, slow with his ears and his heart.

But no one lives forever. The farmer grew old and at last
took to his deathbed. As he lay fighting for each breath, he
knew the end was near. Fear took hold of his heart and began
to taunt him. He remembered all those he had overworked
and the men who had died from ill health on his farm; their
faces reared up to haunt him. He called for the priest to make
his confession and, from sundown to sunup, the farmer made a
catalogue of his wrongs.

The priest looked at the sick old man facing death and
struggled not to show his contempt and dislike. Before he
could absolve the man's sins, the farmer's face contorted and
he coughed, struggling for breath. His back arched and then
he was still.

When his body was buried at Hyssington Church, the
church and churchyard thronged with people. No one could
remember when there had ever been so many people at a
funeral! Of course, they were not mourners, but rather people

from across the county who had come to celebrate and make sure he really was dead.

Though his body was buried six feet deep, the farmer's spirit continued to roam. A black bull appeared as soon as the sun went down, bellowing and roaring, its eyes burning like coals. The bull roared through all the streets and through Bagbury Farm; no one could sleep for fear of it. In the morning the roads would be scarred with hoof-prints and smashed gates, and the well would be fouled.

Something had to be done. That Sunday, the congregation gathered and asked the priest what he was going to do to get rid of the bull. The priest had been expecting the question and knew that, somehow, he would have to exorcise the ghostly beast. It wasn't going to be easy. He sent messengers to all the neighbouring parishes until, at last, eleven priests came to join him, from a young man in his first post to the old blind priest, who had dealt with his fair share of spirits already.

They gathered in Hyssington Church on Sunday morning. The twelve priests knelt in a circle and each lit a candle before them. They began to pray. They prayed all that day. Slowly the sunshine disappeared and a cloud came down over the church. In the distance, they heard roaring and bellowing; the spirit of the Bagbury Bull was drawn into the churchyard. They kept praying and the roaring got louder, as inch by inch, step by step, the bull approached the church. The old blind priest reached down, and, still praying, slipped off his boot and put his candle inside it.

The doors of the church slammed open and there stood the bull, hooves scraping the ground. It was now the size of a big dog; the praying was working. A wind swept around the church and snuffed out all the candles, all except the blind priest's, which was hidden in his boot. As the candles went out, the bull grew larger and larger. The blind priest tugged the robes of the young man beside him and sent him around with his lit candle to relight the others. He called on his brothers to pray harder.

The bull continued to swell, overshadowing the huddled priests filling the church, until the walls groaned under the pressure. There was the grating of stone on stone as the wall cracked and the mortar crumbled. Fumbling with sweating hands, the young priest finally managed to relight the twelfth candle and the bull's growth was checked. The priests took heart, and led by the strong voice of the blind priest, they began the Lord's Prayer, the strongest of all prayers. With each line the bull deflated; to the size of a stallion, then an ordinary

bull, a dog, a chicken and finally a fly. The fly zoomed around the rafters of the church, trying to escape, until their prayer forced him down into a snuffbox.

The spirit buzzed with rage inside the snuffbox. 'Very well, you have caught me. Now lay me under Bagbury Bridge, and every mare that crosses over will lose her foal and every woman her child.'

The priest of Hyssington Church gingerly picked up the vibrating snuffbox and called for the farmhands from Bagbury. They took the farmer's own horses and set off that night for the Red Sea, to cast the snuffbox down to the depths. There, the mean spirit of Bagbury Farm shall wait until the Day of Judgement.

MADAM PIGOTT

I've travelled all around Shropshire, exploring odd nooks and crannies of the county, researching and sharing stories. Whenever I head east towards Newport, I find myself thinking of Madam Pigott and gripping the steering wheel a little tighter.

I was in a primary school in Newport, sharing folklore and history of the area. I was sat with a class of nine and ten year olds, telling them what I knew of the area and asking them if they could tell me any more – if they had heard of any local anecdotes or legends. They listened as I told them about the mermaid in Aqualate Mere; Chocolate Charlie, a boatman who carried chocolate crumbs from the dairy to Cadbury's in Bourneville, coming back with pockets full of chocolate for the children; and Elizabeth Parker, who, when jilted on her wedding day, went back to her house and never came out again, spending the rest of her days at the window looking out, always in her wedding dress.

Of all the local lore we shared, there was one ghost every child had heard of. When I mentioned Madam Pigott, the class exploded into uproar. They all pushed forward, clamouring to tell their story:

'There's an empty house people say she haunts, nobody likes to go there after dark,' said one.

'No, it's not that house; it's the one further down the road with the broken window. My brother dared his mate to tap at the window and he did, and the door opened and they ran away,' another interjected.

'If you look in the mirror and say "Madam Pigott" three times, she'll appear behind you in the mirror, but she'll kill you before you can turn around,' warned a third.

All the children had heard of Madam Pigott. They didn't know why she haunted the town, but they all knew different places she is said to walk, and all of them shared that slight tingle of fear, the prickling down the spine, the excitement and danger of the story that would return to haunt them when next they found themselves alone in the dark.

At lunchtime, talk of Madam Pigott moved to the staffroom. At first the teachers laughed at some of the more outrageous details given by the children, but then they too began to swap tales they had heard of Madam Pigott: how the lane along Cheney Hill is still haunted by her and everyone knows it as an accident blackspot; that the cellar of the deli Wycherley's is said to be haunted by Madam Pigott and the staff only ever go down in pairs.

One teacher remembered coming to the area, young and newly qualified. He was sent with the minibus along the old Chetwynd road to pick up some children from an outing. He thought the other teachers' laughter was because he had drawn the short straw for staying after school. It was only teatime, but it was winter and a dark, wet night. He felt more and more uneasy as he drove along the old road, his wipers battling the brown wet leaves blowing onto the windscreen. He turned the radio on, trying to dispel his disquiet, but the signal crackled and vanished. A prickling ran up and down his spine and his eye caught something in the rear-view mirror.

It was gone too fast to be certain, but for a moment he was sure he had seen a face staring back at him. He was still shaky when he reached his destination, but he smiled at the children and the other teachers, and said nothing at the time. All the same, he took the longer route back into Newport. Only when back at school the next day did he get interrogated by the other teachers, wondering if he'd seen anything strange. He was lucky. It is at night that accidents happen, always when a young man is driving alone. He feels the presence of someone behind him, sees a pale face in the mirror, feels someone else's hands over his own, twisting the wheel from his grip, skidding the car off the road.

People say that it all started with Squire Pigott. He was not the type to enjoy being a country squire and spent most of his time in London. But the squire was no longer a young blade and he knew that he needed to look to his estate. He needed a wife, a well-bred girl to manage Chetwynd Hall and to bear him a son for an heir. He courted a young woman of good breeding and soon the wedding bells rang out.

As far as the squire was concerned, the marriage was a business arrangement. For many young women, it would have been perfect: independence, managing her own budget and estate, no husband under foot to over-rule her decisions – for the squire was far more interested in his life in London than living out in the backwaters of Shropshire.

Sadly, his new bride made a fatal mistake. She fell in love. She waited for her wedding day with sighs and longing. She shared girlish laughter with her friends at whispered snippets of what to expect once she was married. She dreamed of romance, being adored, being shown off to the London crowd.

She was to be disappointed. In the beginning, the squire came home fairly regularly from his business appointments, but once his wife was pregnant and his duty done, he was home less and less, finding his entertainment elsewhere. His young bride was left alone in the great house to be Madam Pigott, learning to manage the daily running of his estate and dealing with servants who knew the estate far better than she did. For the first weeks she mooned over his portrait and eagerly waited for his return, but his visits grew further and further apart and on the rare occasion he was there, he showed more interest in his drinking companions than in her.

The young Madam Pigott pined. Her hopes and dreams withered away, as she dealt with her day-to-day reality. Her loneliness and depression were not helped by a growing sickness as the baby inside her grew. It seemed there was little to her life but duty. Her health grew worse as her belly thickened, and by the time the baby was due she was frail and weak.

With the birth of his heir imminent, Squire Pigott returned home, waiting for the baby to make its arrival. At last the pains started and the midwife was sent for. When the midwife arrived and saw how weak the mother was, she immediately asked for the doctor.

The hours ticked by. Madame Pigott was running out of strength and time. Squire Pigott paced up and down outside the chamber, awaiting the arrival of his son.

Eventually the door opened and the doctor emerged from the room. He wiped his hands on a towel, looked at the squire and shook his head.

Madam Pigott, in a hazy cloud of pain, holding tight to the midwife's hand, heard the doctor's voice through the wall.

'I'm sorry. I've done my best, but time is short. There is a chance I might save one or the other, but I cannot save them both,' the doctor said.

'One must lop the root to save the branch,' was the squire's reply. Madam Pigott heard her husband's clipped tones as he spoke these words. He did not ask to see her.

The door to the birthing chamber opened again. She gave a sob and tried to push herself away as the doctor came towards her. Then there was silence. Neither mother nor child survived.

The next night Squire Pigott was woken by the sound of sobbing and a baby crying. He sat up in his bed, looking around.

Abruptly the noise stopped. He went back to sleep, but twice more he was woken by the crying. The third time he got out of his bed and was drawn to the window. On the moonlit lawn was the form of his wife clutching her baby close.

Each night that Squire Pigott spent in the house, he was woken by the sobbing and crying, until at last it was constantly in his ears. He would wake in the night, sheets wrapped tightly around him as though he were a swaddled baby. Each night, the sheets grew tighter, until he barely managed to free himself and fell choking and fighting to the floor.

Squire Pigott left. He went to London and finally moved abroad. Chetwynd Hall was sold. But Madam Pigott stayed. Each night, at midnight, a wisp of white mist funnelled through the skylight in the roof of the Old Rectory and descended on the breeze, until it came to rest on the lawn in front of the house. The mist coalesced into a sobbing woman, clutching a swaddled infant. The spirit walked through the grounds of the house and along the dark, high-banked lane that went up Cheney Hill. Madame Pigott would sit near the top of the hill, rocking back and forth on the twisted roots of an old tree, combing the hair of her ghostly baby in the moonlight.

If a rider were to come past, especially a man racing for the midwife, Madame Pigott would jump up in the saddle behind him and clasp her hands around his waist. She would try to pull the terrified rider down, clinging and clawing, no matter how the rider tried to shake her off. Only when horse and rider crossed running water would she let the terrified man speed on into the dark, leaving her behind.

At last, twelve churchmen assembled to lay the ghost to rest by reading psalms. The clergymen stood in a circle in the church, the door open. They prayed and the church grew dark. A breeze fluttered the pages; Madam Pigott had arrived. The clergy did not falter, relentlessly chanting the words of prayer, but Madam Pigott's spirit was strong and would not be calmed. The sweat beaded on their foreheads while Madam

Pigott's laughter echoed around the church, mocking them. The wind grew stronger, blowing their hair and ripping the pages from their hands as they tried to read. Exhausted by the effort of such intense prayer, one by one the voices of the clergymen petered into silence.

One lone voice continued. Mr Foy, the curate of Edgemond, intoned the words from memory when the pages were torn from his grip. Strong and firm, line by line, his voice rang out, filling the church. Though his hands began to shake, his skin growing pale and clammy with the effort, gradually he was mastering the spirit. Slowly, inexorably, the ghost's powers diminished. No longer whirling round the roof of the church, but drawn down to the centre of the circle of priests, she shrank smaller and smaller, until there was just a glowing ball of mist the size of a mouse, which Mr Foy scooped up into a waiting bottle.

The spirit was trapped. With his mission accomplished, Mr Foy collapsed and the remaining clergy, recovering from their thrall, gathered around to tend him. After a week of bed rest,

Mr Foy was up and about again, but he had paid a price and never again recovered the strength he had possessed previously. But Madam Pigott had been subdued and the bottle was thrown into Chetwynd Pool.

The townspeople had an interlude of peace, with the ghost trapped beneath the water. Mr Foy grew old and eventually died, aged sixty-one. That winter the land was in the grip of a harsh winter. Some children were out skating on Chetwynd Pool and a girl broke the ice with her skate, the blade of the skate cracking the bottle floating just beneath.

Once freed, Madame Pigott was more active than ever. She jumped onto passing wagons and clung onto carriages. Even in daylight, horses would snort and blow, rolling their eyes in fear if they were forced down Cheney Lane. The light of her presence was seen each night on top of Cheney Hill, and few were brave enough to venture out after dark.

Once again, the required twelve men of God assembled. They arranged themselves in a circle, a candle in front of each and an open bottle in the centre. They began to read the prayers and the spirit flew about in a wild frenzy, snuffing out all the candles bar one. The eldest priest stood firm and urged his colleagues to continue. Wide eyed and terrified, they continued to pray, knowing that their circle opened the doors between worlds. If they were cast into darkness, with all candles snuffed, then the door would be open for the Devil himself to come through and claim them. One by one, with shaking hands, they relit their candles and found the strength of will to keep the flame burning. Their voices grew stronger and the wild spirit was at last drawn in between the candles. As the twelve voices combined in the Lord's Prayer, the spirit shrank and was pulled down into the mouth of the bottle. The eldest priest leaped forward and quickly corked the bottle.

That should have been the end of it. No one knows quite what happened to the bottle. Some say that it was thrown into the Red Sea, others that it was buried deep in Newport

Cemetery. But maybe it has been broken again; it seems her spirit refuses to be trapped, for to this day, stories abound about her and new ones are constantly being told. As the years go by, she still holds tight to the bitterness and thirst for vengeance of a woman spurned and betrayed. No matter how much bravado they may show, there are few Newport lads who would dare go up Madam Pigott's Hill after dark.

Eight

LIFE AND DEATH

THE PRISON CHAPLAIN

They hang us now in Shrewsbury gaol
The whistles blow forlorn
And trains all night groan on the rail
To men who die at dawn.

A.E. Housman

Public hangings were a big event in Shrewsbury. The executions took place on top of the gatehouse of the prison. The Dana, Shrewsbury Gaol, is next to the train station and special trains were laid on for people to come and watch the spectacle. Great crowds gathered outside the gaol, food vendors sold their wares, special broadsheets were printed giving lurid details of the crime and pickpockets came and had a field day. In fact, it seemed the only people who stayed away were the burglars, taking advantage of the opportunity to rob from empty homes.

Shrewsbury's hangman refused to stay in Shrewsbury. Instead he stayed at the Pound at Leebotwood to avoid meeting any of the convicted criminal's family. On the day of the hanging he would walk to the train station (now the builders' supplies), join the crowd taking the train to Shrewsbury, get the train back and stay a second night at the Pound before heading home. He was a quiet, unassuming man and those travelling on the train next to him never knew they sat next to the hangman himself. The perk of his job was to receive the rope used for the victim, and often he sold it for far more than his fee.

Shrewsbury Gaol, more often known as the Dana, was not a pleasant place to be, but it was one of the better gaols in the country. It had the lowest hours of hard labour, though that was perhaps less about charity and more about being able to feed the inmates less and not having to invest in hard labour equipment, such as the crank or treadmill.

The staff at the gaol included the governor, surgeon, task-master, schoolmaster, matron, porter, watchman and six turnkeys, both male and female. One of the most important posts at the gaol was the chaplain. It very much depended when you were incarcerated as to the level of spiritual care you received. Each chaplain had to keep a prisoners' character book. Some chaplains obviously had little hope of repentance or redemption for any of the prisoners, writing long analyses of the various inmates' lack of merit.

It happened one time that a new chaplain was appointed, a young man with a young family, determined to make a difference and bring the light of God into the prison. At first the prisoners thought it was terribly funny. When he came to them and earnestly talked of ways they could change their lives, they thought he was making fun of them. When they realized he was serious, they stared at him in bemusement. But the chaplain's opinion was important: he kept a record of their character; he could be called on as a reference after their incarceration, and he decided how much money they should be allocated when they left the prison. None of the short-term prisoners dared laugh or make fun of him. Those with years of imprisonment ahead, or the hangman's rope looming, did not have the same inhibitions. They laughed at his innocence, made rude gestures he didn't understand and followed behind him with their eyes lifted to Heaven, holding their palms together as if praying, whilst those looking on sniggered.

The young chaplain refused to be daunted and slowly, very slowly, he began to earn their respect. Word reached the inmates of ex-convicts who had given up hope of decent employment and yet, somehow, the chaplain had found them a job. The chaplain visited each prisoner individually, when their front of bravado was lessened, and he would sit quietly and listen. Eventually, one by one, the prisoners began to confide in him. When they found that their fears, worries and confessions were not written up in the prison journal – when word did not inevitably reach the ear of the governor – they began to regard him as a friend. Soon no one dared make fun of the chaplain. Though the chaplain might pretend not to notice, the other prisoners would make sure that the clown was well and truly punished.

As the inmates began to bare their souls to the chaplain, they talked of their families; what they would be doing if they weren't in prison. The chaplain asked each convict if they had one thing they would do if they were free. He did his best to grant each prisoner one wish. One man knew that his mother would be struggling with the winter coming and no one there to chop wood for her – the chaplain went to chop wood. Another prisoner, younger than the chaplain, was in prison during the birth of his first child – the chaplain went to visit his wife and child, giving her a little money and passing on the father's love.

So it went on. He lit candles at funerals, gave Christmas presents to children, and paid a month's rent before someone's wife was evicted. Fortunately the chaplain's own wife was as dedicated as her husband. She forgave him his absences and the money given away. She went with him to help the wives left looking after children on their own, or to support the prisoners' mothers when their grown-up children faced the hangman's rope.

But disease does not discriminate. It takes the loved and the lonely, the innocent and the tarnished all the same. Tragedy struck in the chaplain's house; his beloved youngest daughter was sick. The doctor said she was failing fast and it was only a matter of time. The chaplain went into the prison, but stayed only to do the bare minimum of his duties. After three days of seeing the chaplain pale and drawn, worry etching years upon his face, one of the prisoners stopped him before he could hurry off again.

'Father, what is it? We all know something's wrong, but no one will tell us what's going on!'

The chaplain managed a weak smile and said, 'I'm sorry, Tom, I know I'm neglecting you all, but it's my daughter – she's fading fast. I should have known she was too good for this world. The Lord is taking her back into His arms.'

Tom stood aside and let the chaplain pass, but within an hour every prisoner knew the news.

The next morning the chaplain came to read prayers from the liturgy, but before he could begin, one of the prisoners stood up and said, 'Chaplain, you've done more for me than I ever deserved. You never thought twice about giving a little bit of your life to help my family and I'd be right glad to have the chance to do the same for you. Before God, I promise to give six months of my life to your little girl.'

'Er…that's a lovely thought, Joseph, but I'm not sure that's quite how it works.'

But already another prisoner was standing, offering six months of his life. Some gave weeks and months, but those incarcerated for life were happy to give years away. Listening to the promises, the chaplain's eyes grew bright with choked back tears. At last, each prisoner had spoken and the chapel grew quiet.

'Thank you,' the chaplain croaked. With a shaky voice he continued reading from the liturgy.

When he arrived home, his wife flew to the door to meet him. For the first time in a week there was colour in her cheeks and she threw her arms around his neck. It was a miracle, the doctor said. He had never seen a recovery like it.

That girl lived until she was well up in her nineties and when she did die, she had children, grandchildren and great-grandchildren gathered about her. The story was passed down in the family and was collected from the girl's great-granddaughter.

A riddle:

What man loves more than life,
Fears more than death or mortal strife
The poor possess, the rich require
A contented man desires
The miser spends and the spendthrift saves
And all men carry to their graves

THOMAS ELKS AND THE RAVENS

The Elks family lived in Knockin. They were not rich, but they were reasonably well off and lived in a degree of comfort. They owned their home and were able to apprentice their two sons into the trades they favoured. Mrs Elks loved both her children, but Thomas was her youngest and her favourite. When the boys took a tumble, Thomas always ran to his mama. She would scoop him up into her lap, holding him close and wiping his eyes. Thomas' older brother would bite his lip, blink back the tears and pretend not to feel the pain.

As the years went by, the elder brother grew into a sober young man. He was the one groomed to carry on the family name and home. He courted and married a young woman of good reputation and a year or so later they had a son. Sadly they did not live to raise him. While the child was still an infant his parents died, taken by a fever. Mrs Elks, the orphan's grandmother, was guardian to the child and treated him as her own. With her eldest son dead, she doted on Thomas even more than before.

Thomas was apprenticed as a shoemaker. He did what was needed for his work and in time served his apprenticeship and became a journeyman. But Thomas much preferred life outside of work. He liked to have a drink and to go out on the town with his friends. He was always well-dressed and never seen with the same girl twice. He grew accustomed to living life well beyond the means of a journeyman shoemaker. Any time he found himself short of money, he knew that a quick visit to his mother would replenish his pockets.

Mrs Elks' resources were wearing thin; one smile from Tom and she would ruffle his hair and give him anything. But now Tom's extravagances had used up all her savings and she had little left to give him. The first time she refused Thomas' requests for more money, he ranted and raved, unable to believe that the well had finally run dry. His mother tried to calm him, scraping together what she could, though it was far less than he wanted. Tom took what she had and left in anger. When he calmed down he started thinking. He knew that there was still plenty of money, but it was all held in trust for his nephew. It took time for the idea to form, but once the knowledge was there, he could not shake it from his mind; all that stood in his way was the boy. Once the child was gone, he would be heir to the estate and would have money to do with as he pleased.

Thomas decided on a plan. It was summertime and the corn was high in the fields, just turning from green to gold. Thomas hired a lad from Knockin to entice his nephew into the corn fields to pick flowers from amongst the corn. Thomas met the two children in the fields and sent the hired lad home. He lifted his brother's son up into his arms and carried him to the far end of the field where he had put a pail of water ready. He plunged the boy's head into the water and held the struggling child tight until he grew limp and still. Thomas felt the silence press in around him. The birds stopped singing; there was not even a breeze to rustle the corn. Thomas felt a prickling in the small of his back. He dropped the child's body, certain he had been discovered, that someone was watching. He turned and there was a raven, black eyes in black feathers, staring unblinking up at him. Thomas left the body in the corn and hurried home.

It was not until evening that Mrs Elks began to worry. The child was nowhere to be found and had not been seen for some hours. Messengers went knocking from door to door asking for news of the child, for anyone who had seen him that day, for any hint of his whereabouts.

It didn't take long for the lad Thomas had hired to hear the questions going around the village. He saw the messengers and their worried glances. A sick suspicion quickly took root in his mind and his stomach churned at the part he had unwittingly played. He told his father what had happened and the man took his son to tell Mrs Elks his story.

By now, the whole village knew the news and suspicion was strong against Thomas. The people searched the corn field and there they found the child, the wilted flowers scattered around his body. Thomas had intended to return and bury the child that night. He was overwhelmed by the speed of reaction to the child's absence, and when he realised the worry and anger amongst the whole of Knockin, the enormity of what he had done began to sink in. Before the body was discovered, while the sun still lit the land, he took a horse and fled towards London.

It was a beautiful summer's evening – still, calm and warm – the sun lingering in the west, reluctant to sink below the horizon. But Thomas felt chilled. His skin was clammy and his heart thumped against his ribs. He felt as though there was a shadow hanging over him, and it took him a while to realise that there really was a dark shape following him, a raven flapping overhead. As he looked up, he met the bird's black beady eye looking down at him. Thomas was still for a moment, caught in the gaze of the raven, then, 'Raawk' croaked the raven and dived down at him, its talons clawing at his hair. As Thomas tried to brush and shoo it away, a second raven came down, joining in the attack. Thomas batted them away, but it was a brief respite. As he continued on his way, the two ravens accompanied him, sometimes falling behind or flying ahead, but always in sight.

Thomas was not sure if he was being pursued or not, but his fear kept him careful. When he heard hooves on the road

behind him, he would hide in the fields or trees at the side of the road. Every time he left the road, the ravens would follow, flying between him and the road, croaking and cawing, belying any hiding place.

When at last Thomas could go no further, he hid in a barn and fell asleep to the croaking of the two ravens. His sleep was short due to a fearful farmer turfing him out early the next morning, unnerved by the ravens' racket.

As Thomas travelled on, the ravens kept pace with him, black shadows of guilt, nagging at his conscience. He carried on towards London, fleeing his crime but not the endlessly accusing ravens. At last, in Mimmes, in Hertfordshire he took refuge in a haystack, cutting his way deep within it and pulling the stalks in behind him to block out the sound and sight of the ravens. With their croaking cry finally muffled to silence, he sank into a deep sleep.

Thomas was right to fear pursuit, for he had been seen as he left Knockin. His neighbours pointed the direction of his flight and two riders were sent from the village to apprehend him. They followed him almost to London, until they came to Mimmes and the haystack. They would have ridden past but for the two ravens that were ripping at the hay with their beaks and filling the air with a dissonant, rasping cry.

The two men dismounted to investigate. Hidden in the hay they found Thomas Elks, pale, cold and clammy. He stared up at the two men, then past them to the two ravens. The two black birds regarded him for a moment, then spread their wings and flapped up into the air. He watched them as they shrank into two black specks and disappeared.

Thomas made no effort to resist his capture; in fact his captors said he seemed almost relieved. He was brought back to Shropshire, where he was tried and condemned at Shrewsbury, then hanged on a gibbet at Knockin Heath. It was not until his body hung limp and ragged, and the crowd had dispersed to their homes, that the ravens came back to claim Thomas Elks for their own.

THE SHREWSBURY BLACKSMITH

A riddle:

Guess this riddle now you must
Stone is fire and fire is dust
Black is red and red is white
Tell me now this wondrous sight

There was once a blacksmith called Will. When it came to his work, Will was a man that could be depended on. He understood metal; he knew intimately the many colours of fire, how to get just the temperature he needed; he loved the beauty and solidity of a well-made object.

He had served his apprenticeship and now was a master of his craft, with his own forge. People went to him because he knew his trade well; they did not, however, like him. Will was a surly man. While he was at work he was focused on his craft and did not appreciate being disturbed with idle chatter.

He lived alone, and once the forge was cooling for the night, he would often make his way to the alehouse. The first drink or two would mellow Will, but as he carried on drinking he would become boastful and proud, then disagreeable and ill-mannered; no-one dared to meet his eye for fear of rousing his temper. Will was a big, burly man and no one wanted to give him cause to pick a fight.

One night, Will was woken from his slumbers by a knocking at the door. He blearily got up and unbolted it, to find a traveller stood outside his door with a horse. Will saw instantly that the horse had cast a shoe, and it didn't take long for Will to coax the forge back to the right temperature and fit another shoe to the animal. All the while the horse stood quietly, the stranger waiting patiently by its side.

'Thank you, Will,' said the stranger. 'You have made a fine job. And now it is time for your payment. I am Peter and I pay in no ordinary coin while travelling the Earth. I grant you one wish in return for your service. I suggest that you think hard and choose well.'

Will looked up and the stranger pulled back the hood of his travelling cloak. A soft light seemed to infuse the features of the man who stood there smiling. Will bit back the curt retort that had sprung to his lips, as he realised that the stranger was indeed none other than St Peter himself, travelling the land to keep an eye on the people, preach the gospels and help those in need.

'I wish,' said Will, 'that I might have my life to live over again.' Saint Peter was pleased and granted the wish, thinking that Will planned to use the new life to turn over a new leaf. He was to be sorely disappointed.

The second time around, Will retained all the knowledge from the first time around. He didn't need to focus himself to gain mastery of the forge and metal working. Instead he applied himself to all the dark desires he could think of. He carried on drinking and grew more adept at that, but he also learned new arts such as gambling and debauchery, and discovered all kinds of interesting ways to fund his new habits.

When at last his time came to him, he knew the path that he had set out for himself. He followed the downwards road to Hell, thinking that he would find a place by the fire laid out for him. But when he came to the blackened gates, he found them locked. The imps and demons cowered away from him and would not let him in.

Well, Will was surprised, but he turned his feet to the light. At the gates of Heaven was a face he recognised, not infused with a gentle light this time, but an aura of disappointment and disgust. Saint Peter looked at Will and shook his head.

'But…they wouldn't let me in downstairs,' said Will.

'That is not my concern,' said St Peter. 'I did my best for you, and you wasted your opportunity with not one moment of remorse!'

Will had no choice but to go back down to Hell. Once again the guardians of the gate cowered back, but Will would not move until he had seen their master. Eventually the Devil himself appeared at the gates and with a look of admiration said:

> So, you are the blacksmith who took St Peter's gift and destroyed it! You are a man after my own heart. The problem is that, in two lifetimes, you have learned too much wickedness for me to let you in. I have a certain reputation to maintain. I think you might just be too much competition, even for me.

Will pleaded, begged and flattered, but the Devil would not let him in. All he would do for Will was give him a lighted coal from Hell's fires, to keep him warm as he wandered the earth.

And so, to this day, Will is doomed to wander the earth, his body worn to a wraith. He has nothing left but his coal and his name, for he is still known as Will, Will-o' -the-wisp. He traipses the moors and the mosses, carrying his piece of coal, which is burning still. Wherever there is a bit of bog or marsh,

he tries to lead travellers from the road, enticing them with his light to their doom, to keep him company in the mist.

THE DEATH OF DICK SPOT

All of Oswestry was alive with the news; Dick Spot was dead! Ever since he had first come to Oswestry, stories swirling around him like his cloak, he had been a man of marvels, mystery and magic.

Dick Spot was the conjuror, the cunning man. He saw the web of destiny shimmering around each person and saw what their lives would bring. His spirit flew over land and sea to view the fate of ships travelling the oceans. He could find anything that was lost, from a broach fallen into a fireplace to a maiden drowned in a pool. He could bind horses and men to the spot or make them dance frantically to a tune only they could hear.

Dick was born Richard Morris in Derbyshire, in 1710. He was marked out as different from the beginning by a large black

spot near his nose, giving him the nickname he carried to his grave. He was orphaned young and brought up by his aunt, Deborah Heathcote, a fortune teller. It didn't take long for Dick to learn her skills and soon her talents were dwarfed by his gift.

Aunt Deborah did not like being eclipsed by her nephew. Soon, those that came knocking at the door no longer asked for her, but for Dick. Jealous of his talent and the attention, she would pretend he was out and offer to read their fortune herself. Dick always knew though, and somehow the customer would manage to see him soon enough for his advice. At the age of ten he was already helping to recover strayed cattle and stolen goods, and telling hopeful lovers whether their affection was returned. Dick's answers were not always what his questioners wanted to hear, but, time and again, the passage of time proved him right.

Dick's aunt died when he was seventeen and he made his living as a conjuror. His knowledge was uncanny and he was soon a wealthy man, keeping a coach and livery servants. Dick was always able to make money; he knew which ventures would succeed and the outcome of any race or gamble. He did not need to see customers, but he thrived on the comings and goings, people of every degree coming to ask his aid.

Clients came to Dick as a doctor as well as a fortune teller. For agues and fevers, he wrote on three bits of paper and told the patient to bury them secretly in a field. For other disorders they were asked to burn the scraps of paper instead. In every case, they were told never to look at the contents of the papers, else the remedy would fail.

Dick was as fascinated by mechanical workings as the workings of men and fate. In his spare time he was always tinkering with a new mechanism or design. He invented a clock which worked for two years or more without being wound, winding itself by the weight of the atmosphere. Another he made out of wood for the pub that he owned, the White Horse, in Frankwell. It gained or lost no more than a second in a month, which, for a wooden clock, was an impressive feat. Some of his inventions gave vent to his macabre sense of humour. He designed a chair so that when someone sat down, an enormous skeleton leapt up from behind, clutching its arms around the unsuspecting victim, holding them fast until Dick pressed the spring on the back of the chair.

When Dick came to live in Shropshire, spending his time between Shrewsbury and Oswestry, he was already famous, having had articles written about him in London and Paris.

One day, Dick was enjoying a drink at the White Horse on market day. He was appreciating a sit down and the full house of company. A group of regulars were gathered drinking together, the drink oiling their tongues and giving them a taste for some entertainment. Mr Drinkwater, the wool-stapler, was there, and Mr Crump, the warehouseman, as well as a number of their friends.

'Come on, Dick,' they called over, 'give us some sport!'

'Liven things up a bit for us, will you, man?'

Dick gave them a long look. 'And if I do? If, for example, I make that man outside break his pots? Will you pay the damages?' he replied.

The group agreed and, cheering Dick on, called for more to drink.

Outside the inn was an earthenware man. He had set up his stand by the door and all around him were his plates, pitchers and pots on display. Suddenly the man's eyes widened. He picked up a large stick and began waving and beating it all around him, smashing his wares to pieces. His wife joined in beside him, having first grabbed a flail from a passer-by. The people walking past stopped, open-mouthed, to watch what was happening, and the busy street rapidly jammed up. An undertaker carrying a coffin pushed his way through the crowd and suddenly toppled into the empty space in front of the pot seller. His feet skidded on the broken crockery beneath his feet and he fell to the floor. The lid of the coffin flew open and a large white cat jumped out hissing and spitting, then caught its bearings and sped off. The pot man and his wife raced away after it.

The company in the White Horse watched with mouths gaping, drinks forgotten, rapidly sobering up. The amusement faded, replaced by fear, and they begged Dick to stop. He smiled, nodded his head and turned away from the window.

A little while later, the earthenware man and his wife came back to their stand, looking with dismay at the havoc created. As soon as they were spotted, they were brought inside the alehouse and sat down. Once he had a drink in his hand, they asked the man what on earth had happened to make him break his wares. He described how he had seen a great white bear striding over to his stand, peeing over all his goods, and he had tried to send it away. As he beat it back it turned into a white cat, which he lost while chasing it. He did not know what had caused him to see such things – and now his property was ruined.

The company reassured him that he was not mad or possessed and that his losses would be well repaid. He cheered up
considerably when he realised that he had made a profitable
sale on everything he had brought to market that day. He was
certainly more cheerful than some of the drinking party, who
not only had to pay for the losses sustained, but had been so
scared by the experience that they thought the Devil himself
was coming for them. And so, that day, Dick earned another
nickname: Dick Hellfinch.

One of the most common queries Dick dealt with was the
fate of vessels at sea. For so many merchants and investors,
their fortunes depended on what happened miles away, with
weeks until news filtered through. One day there was a loud
knocking at the door. Dick sat in his study, footsteps rapidly
approaching, the sound of a high-pitched woman's voice getting louder and louder. Into his room burst a woman in full
complaint and Dick's maid, trying, without success, to hold her
back. The woman marched over to Dick, brandishing a newspaper and demanding her money back. It transpired that Dick
had told her some time ago that her future husband was sailing
as ship's surgeon on a certain boat, and here, reported in the
newspaper, was news of the loss of the ship and all on board.

Dick held up his hand to stem the flow of abuse and, at
last, she quietened. He gestured to a chair and she sat to wait.
Dick slowly walked around the room, his eyes unfocused. She
watched in sullen silence, fidgeting on the chair. At last, his
body jerked, his eyes snapped back into focus and he turned to
study the woman:

> You are too rash in charging me with impositions. I have not
> imposed upon you, and although the ship is lost, I can tell you more
> than you have yet heard. All the officers and crew are perished, all
> but that very William Hales, who, in spite of all impossibilities, is
> destined to be your husband. He was miraculously preserved by a
> plank and has got to a rock; he is on it now. I have seen him almost
> dead with fatigue, and he will be very near famishing before he

can get to any relief. He is about two hundred miles off at sea, but he will be in Liverpool within three weeks. He has nothing but the clothes on his back, and will beg his way up. You will feed him, clothe him, marry him and bury him all within a year.

Dick and the lady talked for a while afterwards. She apologized for her hastiness, though she was naturally disturbed by her foretold future. Dick consoled her with the knowledge that she would be happy with another husband after William Hales' death.

Dick, of course, always knew when his own death would be, though he kept the knowledge close until he was near his end. He lay on his death bed, friends and attendants gathered round, everyone speaking in hushed whispers. Into the quiet came a strange rapping from behind the wainscot.

'Do you hear that?' asked one of Dick's friends.

'Yes,' he murmured. 'My time here is determined by the light of that lamp, which will go out before morning.'

His friends sat around his bedside, watching his breath rise and fall, looking up each time the light wavered. Finally, in the dark before dawn, the lamp guttered and died, and Dick's chest lay still.

Though Dick was dead, his legacy lived on for many years. His charms were scattered throughout Shropshire and all the neighbouring counties in England and Wales, protecting houses, farms, animals and people. His prophecies continued to play out as the years went by.

It happened one time that a spirit was loose in the little village of Llanwddyn. It was causing havoc, creating fear and mistrust, causing accidents that were no accidents, and setting neighbour against neighbour as the spirit's pranks spiralled beyond control. There was nothing for it but to call Dick Spot. Some say that Dick read the spirit down, forcing it with his strong will and the Lord's word; others said that Dick tricked the spirit through its vanity; but however it happened, Dick had the angry spirit trapped tight in the quill of a pen. To keep it from escaping, he put the quill beneath a great boulder in the river below Cynon

Isaf and swore that the spirit would be imprisoned until the
river ran dry. The local people named the boulder Careg yr
Yspryd, the Ghost Stone, and gave it a wide berth.

However, the spirit's release came sooner than anticipated.
Liverpool needed water. In the 1880s it was announced that
Llanwddyn and the valley were to be flooded, and in the
process, the river diverted and the Ghost Stone blasted. The
village inhabitants complained to the workmen and the archi-
tects, but without success. The day arrived. A hole was bored
into the boulder and the dynamite inserted. A group of local
inhabitants were gathered at a distance to watch, together with
the workmen from Wales and Shropshire who had refused to
have any part in the operation. The Irish and English workers from further afield, carried on with the demolition of the
stone. The blast detonated and when the smoke cleared and
the dust settled, they saw a pool of water in the cavity where
the stone had been. The water began to swell upwards and
the watchers stared, holding their breath. Out of the water
emerged a large frog. It climbed up onto a broken shard of the

Ghost Stone and sat there, rubbing its eyes with its feet as if it was awakening from a lengthy sleep. For a long time all the workmen stood looking at it, until at last it jumped from the rock and swam away.

The reservoir was completed and Llanwddyn now lies submerged beneath Lake Vyrnwy. As for the spirit, no one knows. Perhaps it was only a frog after all; perhaps it resolved to be less troublesome after its long sentence beneath the rock; or perhaps it is still as mischievous and malicious as ever – a bundle of trouble, free to roam the land, nothing to contain it now that Dick Spot is only a memory.

Nine

A HERO'S TALE

FULK FITZ WARINE

In Great Britain
A wolf shall come from the White Land
Twelve sharp teeth shall he have,
Six below and six above.
He shall have such a fierce look,
Such strength and power,
That he shall chase the Leopard
From the Blaunche Launde.
From the Prophecies of Merlin.

Fulk Fitz Warine, 'the Grey Wolf', was born in the twelfth century. A knight, son of knights, he was born of pride, courage
and honour. Wherever he travelled, stories gathered around
him and his fame grew, but his heart was always in Shropshire;
his lands and family were in Shropshire; his ancestral home
was the white plain of Shropshire, with Whittington at the
centre, lost in a King's compromise.

The boys were out in the practice yard. They rolled around in the dirt like a litter of pups, limbs tangled, wrestling and play fighting, shouting, growling and laughing.

'Alright, alright, that's enough, lads, time to get you working,' announced their practice master, striding onto the yard.

Fulk emerged first from the heap, followed by his brothers and foster brothers. They all knew better than to disobey. They took up their wooden swords and followed the master's steps. Play was forgotten in concentration – all the boys wanted to be good swordsmen, each striving to do better than the others and win praise from their fathers.

Looking down from the tower, their fathers were indeed watching and noting their progress. King Henry I of England and Fulk the Brown were among them. The land was peaceful these days and they were older, more settled. Their restless quest for adventure had been replaced with a contentment to watch their children grow. They spent their nights in comfortable beds now, rather than camped on a battle ground, but everyone still knew their triumphs. The two were great warriors and had fought side by side for years. They had battled against the Welsh Prince Jervard all along the Welsh Marches, quelling the uprisings on the border. The bards still sang of their battle deeds, and all the boys learning the sword outside wanted to be like their fathers. Henry and Fulk both had large broods. Fulk the Brown had five sons: Fulk, William, Philip the Red, John and Alan, while the King had four: Henry, Richard, John and Geoffrey. They were brought up together, along with Llewellyn, who was fostered from Prince Jervard of Wales and betrothed to Henry's daughter, Joan, as part of the peace treaty.

The boys were the distraction of the court, creating all kinds of mischief, executing raids on the kitchen and being hounded out with brooms and frying pans, leaving the cook and maids not knowing whether to laugh or cry. Whenever there was mischief planned, Richard and Fulk would be at the heart of it, always plotting together. Time and again the two were hauled in front of King Henry and Fulk the Brown, facing a combined anger that made grown knights quail. It was not until the two penitent boys were escorted out of hearing range that the King and his friend would release the pent up laughter over the latest escapade.

Fulk the Brown's one regret was that he could not raise his sons at Whittington. Prince Jervard blamed Fulk for his defeat – he knew that without Fulk's leadership, the outcome might have been very different. In the peace treaty he had demanded Whittington, Fulk's ancestral seat, and the King had been forced to compromise to ensure peace. But there was an agreement that, when the time was right, Whittington would go back to Fulk's family. When his boys gathered around him, clamouring for him to tell them stories of battles and exploits, he would laugh and regale them with blow-by-blow accounts of the battles, laughing and joking as they re-enacted the moves. But sooner or later, their father would drift into reverie, eyes clouding with memory. He would gather his children close and tell them stories of Whittington, of its corridors and gateways, gardens and stables. He told them of how, early in the morning, the mist would lie across the land, giving the white plain its name; how beautiful it was when dawn tinged the white mist and made the whole land glow orange and pink. The boys would listen quietly for a while, then one of the younger ones would start to fidget. Their father would shake his head and bring himself back to the present. He would look around at his sons and say, 'Never mind. One day we will ride back there together and I will show you your home, instead of walking it in words! Now surely it is time for your beds!'

He would look at young Fulk and share a smile, knowing Fulk had drunk in every word, then ruffle the hair of the others and pick up the youngest boys, dangling them upside down or throwing them over his shoulders to carry them to bed.

Fulk took after his father. He had the same grit and determination, openness and loyalty. Fulk the Brown's heart swelled with pride as he watched his sons – Fulk always the leader of the pack with the others close behind – venturing off on the latest quest. Wherever Fulk led, his brothers followed like a litter of wolf cubs, tumbling over each other in their fighting and play.

For the most part, the court youngsters got on well together. When they did fall out, they would be at each others' throats, thumping, biting, kicking and shouting, until the protagonists were pulled apart by the other boys or the nearest knight. The lads would emerge sporting bloody noses, black eyes and bruises. But the next day the fight was forgotten and only the injuries remained, to be shown off with pride.

Prince John was different. John let wounds fester; he nurtured grudges. Like a solitary cat, he could patiently wait for an opportunity for revenge, then strike when least expected.

One day, when Fulk and John were still little more than children, they were playing chess. Fulk was winning and John's frustration was building. As Fulk made the winning move, the prince's frustration broke into rage and he flipped the edge of the board up into Fulk's face. Instinctively, Fulk kicked John in return. John fell back, hit his head on the wall and lay still.

'No!' cried Fulk. He fell to his knees and scrabbled over to John, cradling his head onto his lap and rubbing his ears to try and bring him round. Moments later, John groaned back into consciousness. Fulk was full of apologies, but John pushed him away, running to the King to tell him what had happened. The King listened to John's story and eyed him coldly. 'Hmmm… and what did you do, John? Fulk is not a boy to deliberately slam you into a wall without reason,' he said.

'Nothing, Sir, we were playing chess and he, he just exploded!' John tried to stand up straight and resist the urge to fidget. He could feel the blood rushing into his cheeks.

'Really?' The King lifted one eyebrow.

'Yes, Sir!'

'I'm disappointed in you, John. Fulk is not here telling tales against you and I think perhaps he has more cause. I don't like being lied to, John.'

The King sent for John's tutor and ordered him to give John a whipping. Though John's pride was hurt worse than his hide, with every stroke his resentment towards Fulk burned stronger.

Time passed and the boys grew up. When King Henry died, Richard the Lionheart was crowned King and one of his first acts was to knight Fulk and his brothers.

When Fulk the Brown died, Richard confirmed all Fulk's lands on his son, Fulk Fitz Warine. The King was preparing for his journey to the Holy Land and he created a new post, 'Warder of the March', for Fulk, declaring:

> To no one but you can I entrust the March, Fulk. Under your protection, I know the borders will be safe in my absence. When I return, the Holy Land will be ours. There will be new faith, new hope in the land, a shared celebratory peace. Then will I be able to reward your friendship. I promise that Whittington will be yours again.

Though Fulk and his brothers longed to sail with Richard, they made their oaths to guard the country for his homecoming. They returned to Shropshire with their mother, Hawyse, and settled her back in her own manor at Alberbury. Fulk took on his father's mantle, taking control of his estates and establishing his presence on the border.

The Welsh saw the white teeth, like a gaping maw, on Fulk's coat of arms. They nicknamed him 'the Grey Wolf': he was the constant shadow along the Marches, his sharp teeth worrying at their heels. Fulk's brothers were never far away and were his most trusted men and advisors.

It was the life that they had been raised for and they were content, until news arrived from across the seas. Richard the Lionheart was dead; he had been killed in the Crusades. The Fitz Warines grieved the loss of the King they loved as a brother.

Prince John was crowned King and the Fitz Warines travelled to the coronation, still in mourning. Prince John, however, did not look unhappy about his brother's demise. He sat on the throne, the smug look of a cat at the cream radiating from him. He watched Fulk and his brothers with satisfaction as they knelt before him. Each of the brothers took John's hand and kissed the leopard, the seal of his ring, binding their oath of fealty.

Soon after the coronation, Fulk received a message that King John was coming to visit the Marches. King John made his way first to Castle Montgomery to stay with Baldwin de Hodenet, Fulk's cousin.

News travels fast and word reached the ear of Sir Moris, Lord of Whittington. Sir Moris sent the finest gifts he could muster to the King; a white stallion and white moulted gyr-falcon. John was delighted with the richness of the gifts and called Moris to him. The new King took immediately to the ingratiating Moris, a man showing proper respect and defer-ence. The two talked, John lapping up Moris' honeyed words.

As the evening wore on, and the drink flowed, Moris asked John if he would confirm the honour of Whittington upon him, and also his heirs, as his father King Henry had con-firmed the honour, for his lifetime, upon his father, Roger de Powys. John knew full well the history of Whittington – that it had been Fulk's home and belonged to Fulk by right. He knew that his father and brother intended Whittington to be returned to Fulk as soon as possible; he knew that Fulk's father had fought with dogged determination beside his own father, winning back the lands that his father had lost; he knew that sacrificing Whittington had been the only way to bring peace and it was poor repayment for Fulk the Brown's loyalty. A smile spread over John's face. All the boyhood jealousies – every time Fulk had surpassed him on the practice field, every time Fulk had been given favour above him, the King's own son – they all rose to the surface, clamouring for attention. Here at last, in one fell swoop, was his chance to prove his power over Fulk.

John told Sir Moris to put what he liked in writing and within moments, Moris had the deed written out. John pushed his mark, the spotted leopard seal, into the warm wax. Moris smiled and passed him a hundred pounds to thank him for the favour. John smiled and realised he had found the ideal man to be 'Warder of the March'. The two opened another bottle and toasted the deal. In the space of an hour, both Fulk's inheritance and position were signed away.

Word came to Fulk, who was already on his way to the meeting. He could not believe his ears. He hastened his journey, his four brothers riding alongside him. They came before the King to discover that the rumours were true. There sat Moris at the King's right side, smugly smirking. Fulk and his brothers appealed to King John, explaining again Fulk's right to Whittington. Fulk saw the flash of triumph in John's eyes and stopped mid-sentence. He would not beg; he would not give John the satisfaction. Instead he held up his hand to silence his brothers, looked John in the eye and, with tightly controlled fury, said:

> Sire, my family has served you well. I would have risked life and limb for you any time you asked. You are my liege lord. I am bound to you by fealty since I have been in your service, but you fail me both in reason and in common law. I can serve you no longer. I renounce my allegiance to you.

Fulk turned and walked out, his brothers at his heels. The clattering of their boots resounded in the sudden quiet. As soon as they were out the door Fulk lengthened his stride. Without turning, in a voice just loud enough for his brothers to hear, he said, 'Be ready, it won't be long.' The brothers leaped onto their horses and galloped through the gate. Sure enough, pursuit was not far behind. Hoof beats sounded behind them and fifteen of the King's retainers came racing after them to claim Fulk's head. Fulk and his brothers wheeled to face them. The retainers were no match for the Grey Wolf and his brothers, and, within moments, the knights lay dead or dying, save for one who fled to deliver the news to King John.

Fulk and his brothers swiftly made their way to Alberbury to say their goodbyes to their mother, Hawyse. They then fled the country for Brittany.

Hawyse could not believe how her life was turned upside down in an instant. Such a short time ago she had been a favoured Lady of Court, her family gathered around her. Now her husband was dead and her sons across the sea, no longer welcome in the land that she had dedicated her life to. Hawyse was a strong woman; she had survived the sleepless nights of her husband's campaigns; this too she would endure. She held herself with dignity, but there was a brittleness to her – the deep weariness of worry.

King John was delighted how things had turned out. At last he had the power he craved and his revenge on Fulk. He declared Fulk and his brothers outlaws and seized their lands.

In Brittany, the Fitz Warines attended all the tournaments, winning fame and renown, but they were just marking time, allowing the dust to settle. When word came of their mother's illness, they knew it was time to return. They sailed across the Channel and made their way over land to Shropshire, travelling only by night. They were too late. Hawyse, their mother, was dead. All that night they mourned at her tomb.

As dawn came, Fulk rose from his knees, stood in the graveyard and looked out across the white plain of Shropshire, covered in the dawn mist that gave it its name, only Nescliffe breaking free of the cloud blanket. He stood

They BECAme outlaws

watching the sun rise and the haze clear, Whittington slowly materialising out of the mist. His sorrow and grief mingled with anger and resentment.

Fulk's hand tightened around his sword handle as he stared towards his father's beloved home. So this was how Fulk the Brown was repaid for a lifetime of dedication and bravery: his wife left to die in grief and loneliness; his sons outlawed; his home sold for a bribe to his enemies and his name besmirched. Fulk's own slights seemed nothing after the insult to his father. Fulk had never felt hate before, but now it pounded through his veins. King John — his own foster brother — had deliberately heaped such shame upon the name of Fitz Warine.

'It is time to pay a visit to Moris,' Fulk spat out the words.

With renewed determination, Fulk, his brothers and a small band of loyal friends and cousins set out. They hid close to Whittington in Babbinswood, hoping to spy out the lie of the land. Unfortunately, a valet heard the clink of armour, spotted them between the trees and took the news home to Whittington. When Moris heard that Fulk, the man whose birthright he'd stolen, was on his doorstep, he rode out with thirty well-mounted men and a horde of foot soldiers.

When Fulk saw his enemy, rage overwhelmed him and he threw himself into battle like a rabid dog. The Grey Wolf slaughtered his way through Moris' men until he reached Moris himself. Fulk's sword smote down. He believed he'd delivered Moris' death blow, but instead his sword sliced through the horse's saddle and deep into its rump. Moris, with his remaining men, was on the run. The Grey Wolf, teeth bared, raced behind them almost to the gates of Whittington. All that saved Moris were the archers hidden on the battlements. A crossbow bolt whistled through the air and drove deep into Fulk's thigh. Through his red mist, Fulk did not feel the pain and could not understand why he slowed; he howled in frustration as he watched Moris escape. Someone was desperately tugging at him, trying to pull him away. Moris was safely ensconced within Whittington. Fulk came to himself and looked down to see his horse's flank drenched with his blood. Arrows and bolts were raining down; it was time to retreat.

Word spread fast that Fulk was back. King John sent out a hundred knights, paying all of their expenses, promising a large reward for anyone who caught Fulk, alive or dead. The knights roamed the country, supposedly in search of Fulk. Some, however, searched more thoroughly than others. Many headed in the opposite direction when they heard hints of Fulk's whereabouts – some for the sake of respect and old friendships, most through fear of the infamous Grey Wolf.

Fulk and his brothers lived as outlaws; they were raised with princes but now they slept in ditches. They travelled through the land making camp and taking refuge in the forests, visiting towns and villages to feel the mood of the land and monitor King John's movements. Fulk's band swelled in numbers as King John raised taxes, played petty games and took advantage of other men's wives.

Fulk and his band were in Wiltshire, in the forest of Braydon. Fulk's wound was healing, but his temper was not. He was frustrated with hiding, of being cautious and careful. He was weary of sleeping on the ground, spending his nights imagining Moris striding through his home. But one day, a jay blurred over his head and between the branches, its warning call reverberating through the trees. A moment later, one of his brothers appeared by his side shouting, 'Foot soldiers, on the road!'

Fulk and his men silently slipped through the forest to the road. There were two dozen soldiers and in the centre, unmistakably, were merchants. Fulk nudged his brother John forward to find out what the band were up to. As John stepped out onto the road ahead of them, the soldiers stood ready and one man-at-arms charged forward to attack. John neatly side-stepped him and cracked him over the head with the blunt of his sword. After that, the battle was short. The soldiers were taken away from the road, tied up and left with a guard and food. The merchants were led into the forest, where they told Fulk they were servants of the King, taking him the finest goods they could find.

'Tell me true,' said Fulk, 'if you lose this property, on who will the loss fall?'

'Sir,' they said, 'if we lose it through cowardice, or by carelessness, we ourselves are responsible; but if we lose it otherwise – by danger of the sea, or by force, the loss will fall upon the King.'

Fulk's day was looking up. A broad smile spread across his face. He divided the cloth, furs, spices and perfumes amongst his followers. That evening they had a feast and the merchants were the guests of honour. As night fell, they escorted the merchants back to the road, released their guard and sent them on their way. Fulk had a new game to play – something to keep him occupied until his chance should come – to cause the King as much discomfort and pain as possible, while leaving the King's subjects alone.

The merchants and their foot soldiers arrived before the King. They repeated all that had happened, describing how Fulk had taken the King's property. King John was furious. The merchants cowered in front of him, fleeing as soon as they could. King John paced back and forward through his castle in a foul temper, courtiers, servants and soldiers all melting away before him, none wanting to stand in the path of his ire. For a day, no-one dared approach him. At last, in his fury, he sent a proclamation throughout the realm: any person who would bring Fulk to him, dead or alive, would receive a thousand pounds. The King also added to the reward all the lands that had belonged to Fulk in England.

With the stakes raised, the hundred knights that were charged to capture Fulk found new resolve.

Fulk and his company made their way east and set up camp in Kent. One day, Fulk decided his horse needed exercise. He headed out on his own for some much needed respite from the constant noisy banter of the men. Fulk trotted along the empty road, enjoying the morning. The sun was warm on his head, it was a beautiful day.

On the breeze came a lilting melody. Fulk looked along the road and saw coming towards him a young man, a messenger with a wreath of roses about his head. There was a spring in his step as he sang. Fulk felt his heart lift at this rare moment of normality and innocent pleasure.

'Young man, how much for the chaplet that you are wearing?' Fulk said.

'Good sir, to you, not a penny. How could I charge a knight such as you for this small request?!' He smilingly handed the roses to Fulk, who smiled back and thanked the young man with twenty shillings. But the messenger had recognised Fulk. When he came into Canterbury, the hundred knights were gathering, responding to reports that Fulk was in the region. The messenger sold Fulk to them and each of those hundred knights gave him more than twenty shillings in return.

The knights began their hunt. They gathered up foot soldiers, knights and squires, and circled them about the forest, setting them as beaters and receivers to flush Fulk out as a pheasant. Fulk and his band were blissfully unaware of the growing activity around them. At last, Fulk lifted his head.

'Hush! What was that?' he said suddenly. The low note of a horn sounding through the forest called the camp into readiness. The scouts quickly reported that they were surrounded, and Fulk and his companions mounted their horses and prepared for battle.

They fought bravely, cutting great swathes through the men assembled against them, but now everyone knew where they were. The horns sounded and the net of men throughout the forest were all coming to join the fray. Fulk fought with a fierce grin on his face, unleashing all the days of pent up frustration. But then, looking up, with no time to do more than call an unheeded warning, he saw the blow fall on his brother John's head; he saw him sag in the saddle. Before his stricken brother could fall from his horse, Fulk was at his side, lifting him onto his own mount, sounding the retreat. Fulk and his men fled, rapidly pursued. They managed to shake their pursuers temporarily, but soon they could feel the net tightening once again. They abandoned their horses and skulked their way through the forest, from copse to coppice.

Eventually they came to an abbey, somewhere they might finally be able to stop and care for John. The porter saw them coming and hurriedly closed the gates against the battle-marked men, but Alan, the tallest of Fulk's brothers, vaulted over the wall.

'Stop!' said Alan. The porter gave a panicked look over his shoulder and his portly legs ran even faster. With three strides, Alan caught up with the porter and lifted him up by his habit, his legs still racing in mid air. Alan took the keys from him and let his companions in. The band put the monks' habits on over their own garb, then safely locked the monks in the cellar. In the guise of the porter himself, Fulk stepped out into the road, back hunched, leaning on a staff and limping. Already the road rumbled with pursuit approaching. A mob of knights and foot soldiers arrived, pulling to a halt as they saw the monk in the road.

'Old monk, have you seen any armed knights pass this way?' called down one of the knights.

> Indeed I have, arrogant loutish rogues that they were! Seven on horseback and fifteen on foot – and I, old man that I am, stumbled to make way for them on the road, but they paid no attention to me, no. No need to consider a poor old man of God, no, not at all; instead they rode over me as if I was nothing but horse droppings!

'Never fear, friend, you shall be avenged before the day is out!' assured the knight. The mob picked up speed, leaving Fulk in the dust behind them.

Fulk waited, knowing there would be more to come. Sure enough, he saw sun reflecting from steel. Down the road, in

shining armour and on immaculate white horses, came Syr
Gyrard de Malfec with his band of ten knights. They were
always the most impeccably turned out and always at the back
of every battle.

'Oh, look what we have here!' sneered the knight. 'Why,
you are a most fat and burly monk. I thought you monks were
supposed to spend your lives fasting, and yet your belly could
hold at least two gallons of cabbage!' Sir Gyrard turned to
his knights, laughing. Fulk's staff came down on the back of
Sir Gyrard's head. A look of surprise slowly dawned on Sir
Gyrard's face as he toppled off his horse. Sir Gyrard's knights
took one look at Fulk's armed men coming out of the abbey
gates and hurriedly dismounted, dropping their weapons. The
knights were tied up and tossed in the cellar with the monks, a
knife and the keys. By the time they freed themselves, Gyrard's
fresh horses had taken Fulk and his men a good step on their
journey back to Shropshire, to Fulk's aunt at Higford.

Fulk, his brothers and his friends lay low in Higford while
John's head wound was tended. But as John recovered his
health, they knew it was time to move on, before they brought
danger to their aunt. They travelled through the northlands
and to Scotland, but at last, as always, Whittington called Fulk
home to Shropshire.

They made camp in the forest at Alberbury, near the river,
where Fulk could walk up to his mother's tomb and look
across to Whittington. Fulk needed to know what was happening within those walls. He walked back to join his ragtag
bunch of family, friends and followers, and called upon John
de Rampaigne to take a walk with him.

'John, you know something of juggling and minstrelry. We
need to know what Moris is up to. I have asked much of you
already, but I need more. Will you be my spy? Will you venture into Whittington?' he asked. John and Fulk's eyes met and
slowly John nodded his head.

John went into the forest and came back with an innocuous
looking leaf. His companions watched, fascinated, as he dug a

hole, washed the leaf, crushed it, chewed it in his mouth, spat it
into the hole and buried it. Slowly, John's face began to inflate
like a balloon. His cheeks puffed out; his nose, chin and forehead all swelled; his eyes sunk into the flesh and a stain spread
across his skin, darkening it. Their mouths dropped open as
they stared at the sudden stranger, until a grin flashed across
his face, revealing the man they knew. John dressed himself in
old travel-stained garb, slung a box of juggling gear across his
back and set off with a staff.

A juggler arrived at Whittington that night, claiming to be
from the Scottish Borders. The porter let him in and took him
to Sir Moris, who looked up briefly and drawled, 'A juggler,
well, I suppose new entertainment would be welcome. And
what news do you bring from your travels?'

'None, my lord, except that the King's enemy, Fulk Fitz
Warine, is dead. He was killed while committing a robbery at
the house of Sir Robert Fitz Sampson.'

'Is this true?!' said Moris, sitting up on his chair, all traces of
boredom falling away.

'Why yes, my lord, all the border lands are talking about it!'

'Then this is good news indeed, and as the messenger, let me
reward you handsomely!' Sir Moris gave John a silver cup and
asked him to perform. The best barrels in Moris' castle were
breached, the cups overflowed and the whole castle celebrated.

The alcohol had its effect. Even though the juggler was the
bearer of good news and the cause of celebration, some of
Moris' men began to mock him. They made fun of his dark
skin, his piggy eyes and swollen features. They pinched and
pulled his hair and feet. John de Rampaigne did not respond
well to insults. He jumped to his feet, lifted his staff and
cracked one his tormentors over the head with it. His skull
split like an egg; the party ended abruptly. John apologised, he
had only meant to teach the lad a lesson and had not meant to
hit him so hard. Sir Moris let him live, in return for the good
news he had brought, but John was thrown out of the castle
and sent on his way.

John de Rampaigne travelled back across the white plain, his mission accomplished. He sat at Fulk's fire and told him that the very next day Moris would be travelling with a band of fifteen knights to Shrewsbury in his role of 'Warder of the March'.

The next day Moris took the road to Shrewsbury, his head still cloudy from the celebration. As he looked over towards Great Ness, he saw the sun illuminate silver teeth on a shield, and in that moment he knew the Grey Wolf had returned. 'A curse on all false-tongued jugglers,' he muttered, turning his horse's head.

There was nowhere to escape to this time. Moris had no choice but to rally his men and meet Fulk's onslaught. His voice sounded high and thin as he tried to bolster his men, saying, 'At last, Fulk, tonight your head will be decorating the highest tower in Shrewsbury!'

It was not to be. Moris and his men fought with the ferocity of cornered rats, but the battle was short and soon Fulk wiped Moris' blood from his sword.

Fulk sighed in satisfaction as the last of Moris' men fled into the distance. But his eyes soon turned in the direction of Whittington. His heart yearned to return home, but though Moris was defeated, King John still held the throne and Fulk was an outcast.

Instead, Fulk turned west, seeking refuge in Wales. He turned to his childhood friends, Sir Llewellyn, Prince of Gwynnedd, and his wife, Princess Joan. But they were not children any more. Joan was the King's sister and, though Llewellyn's relationships with King John were strained at best, Fulk was not sure Llewellyn would want to test them to breaking by having Fulk in his household. He need not have worried. When Llewellyn saw Fulk he threw his arms around him in welcome.

King John was in Winchester when the nervous messenger arrived and delivered the news in trembling tones. The King sat silently for a long moment; his court held their breath,

waiting for the explosion. Eventually he looked around the
room and said in a very low voice:

> So. Fulk has killed my friend and servant, Moris Fitz Roger, and
> taken refuge with my own sister. I am the King. I rule England.
> I am duke of Anjou and Normandy, and the whole of Ireland is
> under my lordship. Yet I cannot find a single man in my entire
> realm who will avenge me for the damage and the disgrace that
> Fulk has caused me!

King John sent a summons for all his earls, barons and knights
to meet him in Shrewsbury.

Such a gathering could not remain secret. Word came to
Llewellyn and Fulk, who mustered thirty thousand men at
Bala. In addition, Gwenwynwyn, whom Fulk had helped
greatly in the past, came with all his troops to Fulk's side. They
were still vastly outnumbered, but Fulk had always been better
at chess than King John. He knew John had never learned the
stealth of a wolf or the wiles of a fox, always relying instead on
force and numbers.

Fulk knew every inch of the land and he knew which
route John must travel. He made his way swiftly to the ford of
Gymele, near Alberbury, a narrow pass enclosed with woods
and marshes. He instructed his troops to dig out a long, deep,
broad ditch, then to dig through, connecting it to the river
and filling it with water. Beyond the ditch they built and
fortified a palisade. With the river, marsh, ditch and fortifica-
tions, the only way through the pass was on the highway, then
through the ford. Fulk made a hidden path through the marsh
and waited on the Shrewsbury side, with more forces waiting
on the Welsh side, with Gwenwynwyn. The trap was set.

King John and his army came to the ford. He looked up,
thinking how wide the river was, then realised the sunlight
was not glinting off water as he'd thought, but armour. The
battle cry sounded. Fulk and his men attacked the King's
flank. The forces clashed and the air was rent with the sound

of steel against steel, sword against sword. The river and ditch were stained red with blood. For a moment, King John's men were caught in unprepared disarray, frantically trying to hold back the host bearing down on them. Then they rallied. Fulk's men fought like wolves, spurred on by the Grey Wolf himself. At last, with King John's men pressing all around them, Fulk's band retreated along the hidden path, those trying to follow being lost to the marsh. From the other side of the palisade, Gwenwynwyn's men rained down crossbow bolts and spears on the King's troops, until they could barely move for the fallen.

The struggle continued until the light faded. King John watched over the devastation of his army and did not know what to do. He finally admitted defeat and called the retreat to Shrewsbury.

Prince Llewellyn was delighted at the humiliation of the English King. He and Fulk celebrated and Llewellyn formally restored Whittington to Fulk, as well as estates in Denbighshire and Montgomeryshire. With joy in his heart, Fulk returned to Whittington and had the castle restored and thoroughly repaired.

Once again, King John was fuming. Fulk had humiliated and defeated him – again. He wrote a letter to Prince Llewellyn, promising to restore all the lands that the King's ancestors had ever taken from the Princedom in return for Fulk's body. Llewellyn showed the letter to his wife, who instantly had it copied and sent to Fulk. When Fulk saw the letter, he knew it was time to leave. Without Llewellyn's protection he couldn't hold Whittington, and while he was sure of his support, he could not threaten the hard-won truce his father had sacrificed so much for. Until he could make peace with King John, or until John no longer held the throne, they were at stalemate.

With heavy hearts, Fulk, his brothers and his friends left Shropshire and took sail to France. There he commissioned a boat, still determined to punish King John for the injustices he'd suffered at his hands. For a year, Fulk sailed just off the

coast o   provisions for King
John, b   ... alone.

Eventually, Fulk and his companions sailed to shore. They
landed at Dover and travelled inland, leaving the ship and its
captain waiting for them. Sympathy for the outlaws had spread
through the land, and local gossip informed them King John
was at Windsor. During the day they slept and rested themselves; at night they travelled to Windsor. In happier times they
had often hunted through Windsor Forest and easily found a
place to camp and hide.

They had only been in the forest a day when they heard a horn
sounding. The King's hunters and beaters were preparing for a
hunt. Fulk left his band in hiding and set out on his own to delib-
erate his next move. He knew the only way he could defeat the
King was by guile. His first encounter was with an old charcoal-
burner. Fulk greeted him and, taking the opportunity, asked the
charcoal-burner to sell him his clothes and shovel and go and have
a drink on him. The charcoal-burner gave Fulk a suspicious look,
but when he saw the gold coins in Fulk's hand he willingly agreed.

Fulk changed into his disguise and saw to the coals with a large
iron fork used to arrange the logs on each side. Luck was with
him. He had not been there long when he heard people on the
path. King John himself arrived on foot accompanied by only
three knights. Fulk immediately recognized the King and, throwing down his fork, saluted his lord by falling humbly to his knees.

'You, peasant, have you seen a stag or doe pass this way?' the
King demanded.

'Oh yes, my lord, some time ago,' replied the disguised Fulk.

'What kind of an animal did you see?'

'One with long horns, my lord. I can lead you where I saw
it, but I ask your permission to allow me to take my fork? If it
were stolen it would be a great loss to me.'

'Yes, peasant, if you like. Go on and we will follow you.'

Carrying his big iron fork, Fulk conducted the King to an
excellent place from which to shoot. King John had always
been good with the bow.

'My lord,' said Fulk, 'would you like me to go into the thicket and direct the animal to come this way?'

'Yes, indeed,' said the King. Fulk leaped into the thick of the forest, and summoned his band hastily to take King John.

'Be quick, Fulk hissed, 'I have led him here with only three knights, and his retinue is still on the other side of the forest.' Fulk and his band rushed out of the thicket, capturing the King and his knights with barely a struggle.

'Now, Sire,' said Fulk, 'I have you in my power at last. Shall I pass such a sentence upon you as you would upon me if our positions were reversed?' The King trembled in fear, for Fulk was the one person in all his empire who he believed might actually have the audacity and capacity to hurt him.

Fulk stood over the quivering King and gave vent to the years of pent up rage:

Now, John, you shall die. You shall pay for the dishonour you have brought on the name of Fitz Warine – after you knew my father, knew how faithfully he served your father. You have brought even more dishonour on your own father's name – be glad he is not here to see how you have betrayed his promise to my family; be glad he cannot see how the people talk of his son as a lily-livered, tax-raising, womanising tyrant. He must be turning in his grave! As you are about to find out.

Fulk raised his sword above John's head, baring his teeth in a wolfish grin. King John cowered like a child. He cried for mercy and, in God's name, begged for his life. He promised that he would restore to Fulk his entire inheritance and whatsoever he had taken from him and all his friends. Moreover, he would grant him friendship and peace forever. To that end, John pledged to abide by whatever guarantees of security Fulk himself might decide appropriate. Fulk accepted the King's offer on one condition: in the presence of all the knights there, King John must give his solemn word to keep the covenant. The King pledged solemnly, the

lie sliding smoothly from his tongue without a flicker of
conscience or honour.

Upon his return to the palace, King John assembled his
knights and retinue and told them in detail how Sir Fulk had
deceived him. Since his oath was made under duress, he had no
intention whatever to keep it. He commanded all his followers
to arm themselves in haste and capture the felons whilst still
in Windsor Forest. Sir James of Normandy, the King's cousin,
requested that he be placed in the vanguard. The request was
granted; Sir James and his fifteen knights, adorned in white
armour and mounted nobly on white steeds, hastened forward
in quest of fame.

John de Rampaigne was not as trusting as Fulk and had
followed like a shadow behind King John and his knights. He
overheard everything. Fulk's hopes were once again obliterated by disappointment in his foster brother. He concluded
that there was no means of escape open to him other than
to fight. Sir Fulk and his companions armed themselves and
defended themselves against Sir James, killing all their oppo-
nents except four, who were seriously wounded. Sir James
himself they took prisoner. Fulk and his men immediately
put on the arms of Sir James and his band. They mounted the
beautiful white horses and set free their own lean nags. Tying
his mouth so that he could not speak, they dressed Sir James
in Sir Fulk's armour, including the helmet with Fulk's coat of
arms, and rode towards the King. When the King saw them
approaching he recognized the Grey Wolf's silver teeth and
was delighted to see that, finally, Fulk was captured.

Sir James was delivered to the King, as Sir Fulk himself.
Presuming that he was addressing Sir James, King John commanded Fulk to kiss him. Sir Fulk replied that, as he was in
such haste to follow the other Fitz Warines, he had not time
enough even to take off his helmet. Pleased, the King dismounted from his own good horse and ordered Fulk to take
it, as a swifter one to pursue his enemies. Sir Fulk got down
from Sir James' horse and mounted the King's steed. When

he rejoined his companions, they all fled to a spot some six leagues farther away. Safe at last, they disarmed themselves in a thicket and tended to their injuries. William Fitz Warine was sorely wounded. He was cut through to the bone and his breath was ragged and gasping. The brothers gathered round, grieving, sure that William's time was short. William begged them to cut off his head and take it with them, so that King John would not recognise the body, and Fulk and his brothers could flee to safety. Fulk refused. Sure that William was dying, he would not leave his side.

Back at the King's camp, King John ordered Sir Fulk to be hanged. Sir Emery de Pyn, a relative of Sir James, stepped forward and said that he would see to the hanging himself. He took charge of the prisoner and took off his helmet. There inside was Sir James, wide-eyed and biting his gag in frustration. With his mouth unbound, Sir James was at last able to explain what had happened. Emery brought Sir James back to the King and reported what Sir Fulk had done. When the King realised how he had been deceived, he was furious. He swore an oath to stay armed in his hauberk until he had taken the traitors.

The King and his nobles pursued Fulk's band, following the hoof prints until they reached the wood where Fulk was hiding. When Fulk saw them coming, he gave one long howl of heartbreak for his wounded brother, William, then gently laid him on the ground and stood to face his enemy.

The assault began. Fulk and his men fought like cornered dogs. Sir Berard de Blois came up behind Fulk and struck him with his sword on the side, thinking he had killed him. Fulk, however, turned on his assailant and struck back, hitting him on the left shoulder and forcing the blade down, with his sword grasped in both hands. Wounded through to the heart and lungs, Berard fell dead from his horse. But Fulk had bled so much that he slid down upon the neck of his own horse, his sword falling from his hand. John Fitz Warine leapt up behind Fulk and held him steady. With no other option, they fled, leaving William behind. The King and his men rode in pursuit, but James' horses were fresh and bore them away; all that night they rode, until in the morning they reached their ship.

They put Fulk to bed in the ship. John de Rampaigne tended his wounds and they sought safety out in open water. When at last Fulk was revived, he asked where he was and whether he had been taken prisoner. His next thought was for William. No one would meet his eye.

The band took refuge in Brittany, where Fulk spent much time on his own. His eyes were hollow from King John's betrayal and from the loss of William – wounds much deeper than the cut to his leg, which left a lasting limp. When their physical wounds were mended as well as they could be, he made up his mind that nothing would deter him from return-ing to England and ending his struggle one way or another.

Once again they crossed the Channel. They followed King John to the New Forest in Hampshire, where they found him hunting wild boar. This time, Fulk refused to trust John and his word. Fulk and his men captured the King, together with six of his knights, and brought them back to their galley

The King was terrified. He opened his mouth to bargain with Fulk, but when he looked at him, he closed it again. Fulk had aged in the months since he had seen him at Windsor. When John looked at him now, he saw a changed man. There was a cold glint in his eye, a cynicism that had never been there before. John had always been able to use Fulk's trusting nature and belief in honour against him. But now there was a weariness – an emptiness – that frightened John more than Fulk's passionate temper ever had.

It was that fear that saved him. Fulk saw in John's panic an echo of the child, the loner, the boy who had wanted to be part of the pack, but could never quite fit in. Fulk and John talked. Too much had happened for them to become friends, but they came to an understanding and a wary truce. At length, the King pardoned Fulk, his brothers and their sup-porters, and restored their inheritance.

Fulk released the King, keeping the six knights hostage until the truce was proclaimed. This time the King kept his word. He returned to Westminster, assembled earls, barons and the clergy and declared he had willingly granted his peace to Fulk Fitz Warine, his brothers and all their followers; their heritage had been restored, and from that time on they should be honourably received throughout the realm.

Fulk and his companions equipped themselves as richly as they could and set out for London in noble apparel. They knelt before the King at Westminster and surrendered themselves to him, upon which the King returned to them all their rightful possessions in England. They were given a royal reception and were invited by the King to stay awhile with him at court, which they did for a full month. Though his brothers relished being accepted once more, renewing their old friendships, flirting and dancing, Fulk prowled restlessly. Shropshire was calling.

They left the formality, richness and rituals of court to head north. They went first to Alberbury and gathered around their mother's tomb to tell her their stories and sorrows, holding their vigil at her graveside through the night. As morning approached, Fulk wandered away from his brothers. In the early light before sunrise he saw the white mist blanketing the land, the white plain of Shropshire. As the sun appeared above the horizon, pink and orange rays lit up the mist, making it glow with colour, just as Fulk's father had described so many years before.

'Brothers, it's time to go home,' he said.

Fulk Fitz Warine and his brothers rode through the dawn mist to Whittington, to the white castle built on marshy ground. The Grey Wolf returned home at last.

Ten

A SHROPSHIRE TOAST

THE DEVIL AND THE STIPERSTONES

The Stiperstones rears out of the landscape, like the spine of a dragon, and glowers over the surrounding landscape. Large rock outcrops jut up from its back, silhouetted against the sky. There are no trees on the hill, except for a grove of ancient hollies clinging to the north-east slope. The hill is rocky, uneven underfoot, covered in shale and scree. Bracken, heather and whinberries hug the scant soil, providing cover for red grouse. Above, the buzzards soar upwards and the lapwings give their forlorn 'peewit, peewit, peewit'.

On summer days with clear skies, the Stiperstones is a beautiful place and families come with picnics to go whinberry picking. But even in summer, the weather can change in a heartbeat; a clear sky can suddenly turn brooding and overcast, a cold wind and a shiver calling a retreat to home. In winter, the Stiperstones can be a bitter, bleak place, with ice-clad shards of stone piercing through a shroud of snow.

There are many stories associated with the Stiperstones. All agree that the Stiperstones is a portentous place – a place to be wary of.

If anyone dares to sit on 'the Devil's Chair', they will instantly trigger a thunderstorm. If someone is brave or foolish enough to spend the night at the foot of 'the Devil's Chair', they will be dead or a poet when morning comes. I've heard several tales of people trying it, in the light-hearted versions – they always run home long before the night is over. But there are sadder tales too; stories of hikers found dead from hypothermia.

The Stiperstones is where all the bad things meet: witches, boggarts, ghosts, bogles, remnants – all presided over by the Devil himself. Once a year, on the longest night, they gather to swap stories of their achievements over the past twelve months and plan their revels for the coming year.

Seven birds, brothers born at the beginning of time, roam the Stiperstones, but one brother is separated and lost, doomed to be alone until the end of time. The birds are the seven whistlers, named for their whistling cry. Six birds search the Stiperstones, calling for their brother, but the day they find him the world will end. It is bad luck to hear the whistlers' cries.

A few years ago, I was asked to accompany some journalists to the Stiperstones. Halloween was looming; a famous horror novelist had written his latest book in Shropshire and so the journalists came to write about the dark side of Shropshire. The Stiperstones was naturally on their agenda. I wasn't completely convinced it was a good idea to go up the Stiperstones in the dark, but we weren't going on the night of Halloween itself and the promise of a pint and a bowl of whinberry crumble in the Stiperstones Inn was enough to dispel my forebodings!

We left late and it was nearly ten o'clock when we arrived at the base of the Stiperstones. It was a clear night, and looking up from the car park we could see the shadowy stones, black against a deep blue velvet sky. We began to climb the hill, feet slipping on the scree. We were less than half way up the slope when the mist came down. It dropped like a curtain, ten feet or so from where we stood. The stones vanished behind the cloud. I refused to climb any further and began to tell the stories of the hill where we stood. As I explained the old myth of the seven whistlers, a low, soft whistle came from the whinberry scrub. The journalists laughed, thinking I'd set it up. I knew I hadn't.

With slightly shaky knees, I told them the story of the Devil and the Stiperstones to explain why I wouldn't take them into the mist.

Long, long ago, when the world was new, a prophecy was made. Whispered on the breeze it passed from father to daughter, mother to son, friend to friend. It passed from mouth to ear, until it reached the ear of the Old Gentleman, Uncle Joseph, the Devil himself. The prophecy told that if ever the Stiperstones should sink into the earth, Shropshire, and England, would be ruined.

The Devil smiled; there are a lot of souls in England. Quick as thought he made his way to the top of the Stiperstones, triumphantly looked out across the county, lifted one hoof and pounded it down. Nothing happened. No grinding stone, no sinking earth; the hill did not even shudder. He jumped into the air and came crashing down with both hooves. Nothing. He took a deep breath, crouched down, leaped as high into the air as he could and thundered down onto the ground. Still the ground withstood him. He pounded up and down until dusk gathered around him, and still nothing happened. The Devil mopped his brow and collapsed onto a rocky outcrop on the top of the hill to catch his breath. The heat from his body seared the rock into the shape of a chair around his body, and it has remained 'the Devil's Chair' ever since.

The Devil couldn't understand it. With his strength and power, the stones should slip into the earth like a knife into butter, but the stones stood firm.

However, one thing the Evil One has learnt since he was cast out is patience. The seven years he offers to bribe a tempted soul pass for him like a breath on the wind. With a prize such as the destruction of England at stake, he was prepared to wait, to plan and to work. Over the years, in spare moments, he came back to the Stiperstones to sit in the chair he had made and try to push it down with the weight of his malevolence.

One day the Devil was down in Hell and a terrible stench crept into his nostrils; a foul odour that made his demons choke and retch. Somehow, fresh air was leaking into Hell. He surveyed the roof of Hell and there he saw it; a crack – a thin, hairline crack – but a crack none the less. When he saw where it was he smiled, for it was along Hell's Gutter, the long valley that lies between the Stiperstones and the Long Mynd. At last the hill was beginning to loosen!

Still, something would have to be done about the smell. He made his way to the Stiperstones to inspect the crack, looking around to see if there was anything handy to plug the leak. There was nothing but heather and whinberries, nothing that would stand up to the sulphurous fumes. Then he had an idea. The giants of Scotland and Ireland had formed a truce; they had stopped warring and were building a bridge of friendship – a causeway between the two lands. Peace was the last thing the Devil wanted! He would take the stones from the half-built causeway and use those, stirring up mistrust and plugging the gap at the same time. He flew up into the air towards the Irish Sea. He gathered an armful of rock, and brought it back to the Stiperstones. He let fall his load and the rocks lay scattered on the ground, lonely pebbles in a sea of green grass. It was going to be a long day. He traipsed backwards and forwards, backwards and forwards, carrying load after load. At last, on one trip, he noticed an orchard being harvested. There were men up in the trees throwing down apples, while the women stood below, catching the apples in their aprons.

'That's it!' thought the Devil, 'I need an apron.'

He swooped down into the next field of cattle, took four of the plumpest, skinned them and cobbled the skins together into an apron. It was a brilliant idea – he was able to carry ten times as many stones on that journey. But by the time he reached the Stiperstones, he regretted his ingenuity. Beads of sweat stood out on his forehead, his arms ached and his skin was scorching hot. But instead of dumping his load as soon as he got to the valley, he struggled to the top of the hill and collapsed into his chair, hoping the extra weight of the rocks would help push the hills downwards. Slowly he recovered and looked around. The hill still stood as it had always stood. He tipped his weight forward and then forced it back down onto the chair, but nothing happened. He lifted himself a bit further and thumped back down – still the hill withstood him. Finally his patience snapped and he jumped high into the air, coming hurtling back down onto the rock. It wasn't just his patience that snapped; so did the apron strings. The stones inside the apron smashed and scattered in all directions, littering the top of the hill. The Devil let out a howl of fury, threw down the tattered remnants of the apron and stormed away in a rage.

But the Devil couldn't keep away for long. The failure nags at him. Whenever he's passing through Shropshire, he returns to sit on his chair, still trying to force the rock downwards. As he sits there, he sees the scattered scree on the ground and the smell of sulphur drifts upwards from the unfilled leak. The memory of his failure returns to taunt him and obscure his thoughts. The clouds in his mind call the clouds and the mist of the sky to gather around him. To this day, whenever the Stiperstones is hidden in mist, everyone knows that the Devil is sat on his chair and the summit is to be avoided.

What the Devil doesn't understand is that he isn't just fighting the hill and rocks. The people of Shropshire are steadfast, sturdy and strong. The land relies as much on them as they rely on the land. As long as there is one person in Shropshire with a love of the land, the hills and rivers, the moors and meres, the stories and stones – one person with no room for the Devil in their heart – then the Stiperstones, Shropshire and England are safe, no matter how long the Devil sits brooding on his chair.

As the story came to a close, we looked once more at the thick wall of mist and then began our descent. The moment we started downhill, the cloud lifted and 'the Devil's Chair' was once again silhouetted against the sky.

SOURCES AND NOTES

THE MAKING OF THE WREKIN

Sources:

Current oral folklore – I have heard versions of this story all my life!

Burne, C.S. (ed.), *Shropshire Folklore: A Sheaf of Gleanings*, from the collections of Georgina F. Jackson, 1883, p. 2–3

Notes:

The most commonly known story of the making of the Wrekin, involves a giant bringing a mountain on a shovel to dam the River Severn and flood Shrewsbury. Fortunately for Shrewsbury, the giant misses his way and ends up lost in the dark near Wellington. He asks for directions and is tricked by a cobbler emptying a sack of shoes he is taking home to mend; the cobbler declaring he has worn them all out on his way from Shrewsbury. The giant decides to give up and go home, dumping his spade full of earth down where he stands – and so the Wrekin was formed. Where he cleaned his boots against the blade of the spade, the Ercall, the smaller hill alongside, was made.

I decided to include this version because, though people may not know the story, everyone around Wrekin knows about the giant. Children commonly point out the shape of the giant's body in the hill. When the telecommunications mast was erected on the summit of the Wrekin, they chose the right spot to enhance the form of the giant and make all Shropshire teenagers giggle. In *Shropshire Folklore*, Charlotte

Burne says that the giant's body made the Ercall, rather than the Wrekin; that he is still alive, though blinded, and in the dead of night you may sometimes hear him groaning. While this is a lovely image, it has been forgotten in local memory and it is always the Wrekin itself that has been pointed out to me.

The Needle's Eye has always been a challenge to the young. As teenagers climbing the Wrekin, we would spurn the winding slope of the main path and attack the steep, shaly bank up to halfway house – only possible by running full tilt. Reaching the top before any accompanying adults, we would make straight for the Needle's Eye, to climb, clamber and squeeze through the narrow gap. In Charlotte Burnes' time, every young maid was supposed to scramble through the passage, with her young man standing ready the other side to greet her and claim a kiss. Any girl turning and looking back would never be married.

Severn

Sources:

Burne, C.S., *Shropshire Folklore*, op. cit., p. 415, 584

Grice, F., *Folk Tales of the West Midlands*, Thomas Nelson & Sons, 1952, p. 31

Regia Anglorum, 'Fishing in Early Medieval Times', www.regia.org/fishing.htm

Rogers, L., 'Sabrina and the River Severn', www.whitedragon.org.uk

Rust, M. (Oral source – heard from coracle makers and fishermen at The Boat, Jackfield)

Tongue, R., *Forgotten Folktales of the English Counties*, Routledge & Kegan Paul, 1970, pp. 28–30

Notes:

This is obviously a story that has travelled up and down the river. A coracle is a small rounded boat made of hide, stretched over a wooden frame; it is light enough to be carried on a man's back. Although there are plenty of bridges across the river these days, there are still coracles to be found on the Severn, with an annual coracle regatta held in Ironbridge each August bank holiday. Until 1979, Shrewsbury coracle maker Fred Davies, and his nephew John, used to be on standby for all of Shrewsbury Town's football games, their job to rescue the football when it was kicked into the river. It was Fred who initially passed on his coracle-making skills to the Greenwood Trust in Ironbridge. Other coracle makers have since contributed their knowledge and the Greenwood Trust regularly run teaching courses to keep the skill alive.

SAINT MILBURGA

Sources:

Burne, C.S., *Shropshire Folklore*, op. cit., pp. 416–419

'Houses of Cluniac monks: Abbey, later Priory, of Wenlock', *A History of the County of Shropshire: Volume 2*, 1973, pp. 38–47, www.british-history.ac.uk/report.aspx?compid=39923

Mumford, W.F., *Wenlock in the Middle Ages*, Wildings of Shrewsbury Ltd, 1977, pp. 5–6, 147–149

WILD WILL OF WENLOCK

Sources:

Fairweather, C. (tr.), Salop Wenlok, Rotuli hundredorum, temp. Hen. III & Edw. I in Turr' Lond' et in Curia Receptae Scaccarii Westm. asservati, volume II, House of Commons, 1818, (Shropshire Archives: qC63)

'Much Wenlock', *A History of the County of Shropshire: Volume 10*, 1998, pp.399–447, www.british-history.ac.uk/report.aspx?compid=22888

Mumford, W. F., *Wenlock in the Middle Ages*, op. cit., pp. 21–23

Peele, M., *Some Shropshire Stories*, 1980, pp. 3–6

Notes:

There is still more to this story to be found! From an initial throwaway comment, the story has unravelled to reveal a web of intrigue, bullying, bribery and corruption. As always, research is a never-ending task. By including the story as it is, I hope readers with other parts of the jigsaw will get in touch.

HUMPHREY KYNASTON

Sources:

Burne, C.S., *Shropshire Folklore*, op. cit., pp. 15–18

Gough, R., *The History of Myddle*, Futura, 1981, pp. 27–28

Shropshire Notes and Queries, 12 and 19 January 1894

Notes:

Humphrey Kynaston was the last tenant of Myddle Castle and was outlawed in 1491. Kynaston's cave still exists at Nescliff, together with the worn away sandstone steps. You can peer inside, but the cave is padlocked to protect three species of bats that now live there.

IPPIKIN

Sources:

Burne, C.S., *Shropshire Folklore*, op. cit. p. 15
Pugh, K. & Waring, S. (Oral sources)

MAJOR'S LEAP

Sources:

Burne, C.S., *Shropshire Folklore*, op. cit., p. 14
Stratton, C. (Learning Officer, National Trust, Shropshire Hills)

Notes:

In another version of Major Smallman's escape from Wilderhope, his getaway was via the garderobe. I wish this was true, but Chris Stratton assures me it is highly unlikely. The structure of Wilderhope, however, does suggest a blocked up stairwell winding around the chimney – a window can be seen from outside that does not correspond to any room and would have lit the passageway.

THE LOST BELLS OF COLEMERE

Sources:

Burne, C.S., *Shropshire Folklore*, op. cit., pp. 67–68
Oral folklore

Notes:

Answer to riddle: Church bells

THE WOMEN OF WEM

Sources:

Bracher T. & Emmett R., *Shropshire in the Civil War*, Shrophsire Books, 2000, pp. 27–28

Garbet, S., The History of Wem, 1818, www3.shropshire-cc.gov.uk/roots/places/wem/garbet/wem36.htm

Mythstories Museum of Myth and Legend, Wem, Shropshire

Woodward, I., *The Story of Wem and its Neighbourhood*, Wilding & Son, 1952, pp. 21–25

BETTY FOX AND THE TREASURE

Sources:

Burne, C.S., *Shropshire Folklore*, op. cit., pp. 263–264

English Heritage website:

www.english-heritage.org.uk/daysout/properties/wroxeter-roman-city

Notes:

In 1859, a few years after this story took place, excavating work began on the baths at Wroxeter. Betty's son briefly worked on the dig. He never followed orders, but would be found digging somewhere entirely different to where he had been directed. When asked what he was doing, he always said he had dreamed of finding treasure. The motif of following a dream dreamt three times to discover a treasure is common throughout England and Scotland, the most famous example being 'The Peddlar of Swafham'. This version is Shropshire's own unique variant.

NELLIE IN THE CHURCHYARD

Sources:

Mythstories Museum of Myth and Legend

Woodward, I., *The Story of Wem*, op. cit., pp. 63–65

The Wenlock Devil

Sources:

Brookes, Dr W.P., in 'The Wenlock Agricultural Reading Society
    Minute Book', Wenlock Olympian Society Archives
Gaskell, C.M., 'Old Wenlock and its Folklore', 1894, pp. 259–267
Rust, M. (Oral source)

Notes:

There are at least two versions of this story featuring two different murders. Both versions converge to agree on the court case details: namely, the bootprint; the defendant publicly declaring, 'If I did this foul deed, may the Devil take me,' and the industrial accident with the machinery named for the Devil.

Until recently, Much Wenlock held its own court records, but these have now been moved to Kew. Without the aid of a definite date or defendant's name, I have not been able to track down the court records, if indeed they do exist. If anyone else finds them I would love to hear about it!

Nanny Morgan

Sources:

Burne, C.S., *Shropshire Folklore*, op. cit., pp. 160–162
Gaskell, C.M., 'Old Wenlock and its Folklore', op. cit., p. 259–267
Pugh, E. (Oral source)

Notes:

Nanny Morgan is still a well-known name along Wenlock Edge. I have included only a short story here, based on a description of her house from Catherine Milnes Gaskill and the queries she commonly received as described by Charlotte Burne. Few complete stories have survived, but everyone remembers that she was a witch, and also how she died. She was murdered on 12 September 1857 by her common law husband, thirty years her junior. The initial murder report and magisterial investigation were printed in *Eddowes's Shrewbury Journal* on 16 and 23 September 1857. Dr William Penny Brookes, of Olympic fame, examined the body at the scene and performed the post-mortem. Her murderer, William Davies, claimed that he was held in thrall by her and that murder was his only way to escape.

Nanny Morgan is restless in her grave and haunts the Stretton Westwood crossroads. Sometimes, as cars drive through, the radio crackles and goes quiet, the car stalls and the driver is left in silence, engine and all electrics dead. Then suddenly the car roars back into life. Rumour has it that part of a local policeman's training is to be to be sent out alone to patrol Nanny's crossroads, to see how he copes!

Tom Moody

Sources:

Broseley and its Surroundings…, illustrated by John Randall, 1879,
   reprinted in 2001 with notes by Broseley Local History Society

Nimrod, Hunting Reminiscences…, 1843, published by R. Ackermann,
   digitized by University of British Columbia Library, www.archive.
   org/stream/huntingreminisce00nimr_djvu.txt

Palmer, R., The Folklore of Shropshire, Logaston Press, 2004, p. 214

The Fox's Knob

Sources:

Mythstories Museum of Myth and Legend

Nimrod, Hunting Reminiscences, op. cit.

Oral folklore

The Stolen Cup

Sources:

Burne, C.S., Shropshire Folklore, op. cit., pp. 25–32

Rust, M., & Guest, J. (Oral sources – heard from the telling of foresters
   in the Forest of Dean, in particular Joe Guest)

Notes:

At the time of this story, Sudeley was held either by the Earl of Hereford, Ralf de Mederatinus, or his son, Harold de Mederatinus. William the Conqueror allowed Harold to keep the manor, but took away his title of Earl.

Godfrey Hollow is not named after someone called Godfrey; it would have originally been 'God free Hollow', as a haunt of the Fair Folk.

The Hound on the Hill

Sources:

Burne, C.S., *Shropshire Folklore*, op. cit., p. 104

Clowes, V., 'Breaking the Silence', Mythstories Recordings Archive, 1994

Kean, J., & Lewis, M., 'Edric Still Rides', Mythstories Recordings Archive, 2000

Palmer, R., *The Folklore of Shropshire*, op. cit., p. 34, 124

Tongue, R.L., *Forgotten Folktales of the English Counties*, op. cit., pp. 80–81

Notes:

The Wild Hunt rides whenever war is coming, heading out to meet the enemy, the number of hounds in front of Edric indicating how many years the war will last. When he is not needed he sleeps with his men beneath the Stiperstones and used to make a knocking sound to guide the miners to the best lodes. When a personal disaster approaches he is not seen, but heard.

Vera Clowes described a time her mother and aunt had been visiting:

> It was dusk when they set off home. They stood on the main road waiting for the bus to come and pick them up…Suddenly they heard a herd of cattle, coming down the road. They got up on the bank, under a holly bush. The cars were still coming down, a motorcycle now and again, but nobody seemed to hear anything, only them. It got nearer and nearer and they could feel the breath of the animals and hear the whooping of the men on the horses as they went past. They knew it was Wild Edric and they were terrified. Eleven of their family died in the next twelve months.

Edric is not always a bad omen; he is a protector of the land. The most recent sighting I know of was by Jon Kean. When his land at Tankerville was under threat, he was drawn to a barn on his farm. In his words:

I was looking at a very tall strong figure, a black silhouetted figure
with a helmet and a shield, a spear and a cloak. I got no sense of fear...
quite the opposite, I got a feeling of strength, I got a feeling [that] the
Being [was] on guard and the Being [was] telling me everything was
going to be ok, and indeed it was.

THE ASRAI

Sources:
Oral folklore
Tongue, R., *Forgotten Folktales of the English Counties*, op. cit., pp. 24–25

Notes:
Answer to the riddle: Water
They say that after Noah's great flood, it took time for the water to drain
away. But slowly islands began to appear in the world of water – the
Stiperstones, the Long Mynd and all the Shropshire hills. Bit by bit the
land came back, green and fertile. But the water never entirely drained
away. It left meres and pools, moors and mosses. And the water in these
meres is the same water that was left all those years ago, for there are no
streams in and no streams out; the only way the water changes is by the
wind, the sun and the rain.

The story is not far from the truth. The meres were formed in kettle
holes left by glaciers during the last Ice Age. There are meres throughout
Shropshire, but they are mostly clustered together in North Shropshire
as seven sister meres: Ellesmere, Croesmere, Kettlemere, Blackmere and
Whitmere, Newton Mere and Colemere.

They are steep-sided and deep. Nearly all the meres are reputed to be
bottomless. There is an anecdote in *Shropshire Folklore* of a gentleman
riding down the lane between Kettlemere and Blackmere, and asking a
boy he met, as he pointed towards Kettlemere, 'My lad, can you tell me
the name of this water?'

'Oh, aye, sir, it's Kettlemar.'

'How deep is it?' quizzed the gentleman.

'Oh, it's no bottom to it, and the t'other's deeper till that, sir!'

Morwen of the Woodlands

Sources:

Jones, E., *Folktales of Wales*, Gomer Press, 1988, p. 57

Mythstories Museum of Myth and Legend

Mrs Ellis

Sources:

Oral folklore

Burne, C.S., *Shropshire Folklore*, op. cit., pp. 69–72

The White Lady of Oteley

Sources:

Burne, C.S., *Shropshire Folklore*, op. cit., p. 77

Mythstories Museum of Myth and Legend

Oral folklore – this story is a collage of snippets heard from various
    people in Ellesmere

Notes:

Scattered across the Shropshire and the Welsh borders are the haunts of
several White Ladies. They are ephemeral, beautiful, unearthly and dan-
gerous. They are always connected with water – to a pool, lake, river or
mere.

Oteley Hall is a private residence, so I jumped at the chance of having
a nose round on an 'Open Gardens' event. After asking around, I found
the chimney, partially overgrown now. I took many photographs, but
when the film was developed the photographs of the chimney, though
recognizable, came back streaked and over-exposed. The rest of the film
was ruined. I'm not the world's best photographer and I'm sure there are
plenty of explanations, but it did give me pause for thought!

The Boogies and the Saltbox

Sources:

Burne, C.S., *Shropshire Folklore*, op. cit., pp. 45–49

Notes:

The belief in household spirits is common throughout the world. In England and Scotland there is a common story of a brownie attached to a house or farm, who is helpful when treated well and the place run respectfully, but destructive when disregarded. The brownie expects a bowl of cream each night, but is insulted and leaves if thanked (perhaps the most famous version is 'The Elves and the Shoemaker'). There are several examples of boggarts who wreak havoc and chase a family away from a farm. Usually the family are all packed up, their carts rattling down the road, and a neighbour greets them and asks if they're moving. A little voice responds from the back of the cart, 'Aye, we're flitting.' The family realises the spirit is moving with them and gives up and goes home. This Shropshire variant is the darkest I have come across and gives an insight into the fear, belief and distrust most people had towards the realm of fairy and its denizens.

THE ROARING BULL OF BAGBURY

Sources:

Burne, C.S., *Shropshire Folklore*, op. cit., pp. 107–111
Oral folkore

Notes:

It seems wherever you go in Shropshire there is a story of a spirit being exorcised into a bottle or snuffbox. The trapped spirits are buried or hidden under church flagstones, in cemeteries, in pools, or, most often of all, thrown into the Red Sea to await Judgement Day. There are similar stories all along the Welsh Borders, but I am not aware of such a profusion of these legends anywhere else. Most follow a similar pattern to the Roaring Bull of Bagbury and Madam Pigott, but in Ludlow there is the story of 'Tommy and the Ghost', where the cunning man, Tommy, pretends not to believe that the spirit came in through the keyhole and tricks the ghost into the bottle to prove how small it can be.

MADAM PIGOTT

Sources:
Burne, C.S., *Shropshire Folklore*, op. cit., p. 124
Oral folklore

THE SHREWSBURY CHAPLAIN

Sources:
Rust, M. (Oral source, heard from a farmer in The Swan at Munslow)
Shrewsbury Prison 1500–1877 (Shropshire Archives ref: D 34.7 v.f.)
Shropshire Routes to Roots: www.shropshireroots.org.uk

Notes:
Answer to the riddle: Nothing

THOMAS ELKS AND THE RAVENS

Sources:
Gough, R., *The History of Myddle*, op. cit., pp. 65–66,

Notes:
Ravens following a murderer until they confess or are found out is a motif found along the Welsh Borders. This is a particularly vivid version.

THE SHREWSBURY BLACKSMITH

Sources:
Burne, C.S., *Shropshire Folklore*, op. cit., p. 34

Notes:
Answer to the riddle: Coal burning
There are many versions of this motif; a character ruining their chances of entering either Heaven or Hell and being doomed to roam the Earth for eternity. In folklore, this is the worst fate for a soul; it is worse not to have a designated place than to be sent to Hell. In typical Shropshire fashion, this is a particularly bleak version of the story – often in these

stories the character has outwitted the Devil; he has used his wishes to trick the Devil so that he is trapped in a bag, or an apple tree, or a rocking chair, and is forced to stay there until the main character frees them, and this is why the Devil won't let them into Hell – rather than for their sheer wickedness!

THE DEATH OF DICK SPOT

Sources:

Old Acquaintance, *The life and mysterious transactions of Richard Morris. Better known by the name of Dick Spot...*, ESTCID:T089727, ECCO Print Editions, reproduction from British Library

Owen, Rev. Elias, M.A., F.S.A., *Welsh Folk-lore...*, 1887, eBook transcribed by Les Bowler, www.freefictionbooks.org/books/w/15740-welsh-folk-lore-by-elias-owen

FULK FITZ WARINE

Sources:

Kelly, T.E. (tr.), 'Fouke le Fitz Waryn', originally in *Robin Hood and Other Outlaw Tales*, S. Knight & T.H. Ohlgren (ed.), Medieval Institute Publications, 1997, www.lib.rochester.edu/camelot/teams/fouke.htm

Mythstories Museum of Myth and Legend

Wright, T., *The history of Fulk Fitz Warine, an outlawed baron in the reign of King John*, edited from a manuscript preserved in the British Museum, 1885, www.archive.org/details/historyoffulkfitoowriguoft

Notes:

Thomas Kelly quotes Sidney Painter describing a medieval romance as 'a weird mixture of accurate information, plausible stories that lack confirmation, and magnificent flights of pure imagination.' This is an excellent description of the romance of Fulk Fitz Warine. In my retelling of Fulk, I have concentrated on Fulk's relationship with King John and used that as my central thread. The original romance has many fantastic stories and episodes within it, including the story of his father and grandfather, how Whittington first came to the family and of how he rescued maidens, dragons, battles and tournaments. There just wasn't space here, but if you'd like to know more about Fulk there is plenty more to discover!

Fulk was pardoned in November 1203, he recovered Whittington and remained in the King's peace until joining the baronial rebellion in support of Magna Carta, in 1215. He was not reconciled to the King until 1217, and died in about 1256–7.

THE DEVIL AND THE STIPERSTONES

Sources:
Burne, C.S., *Shropshire Folklore*, op. cit., pp. 4–5
Oral folklore

Notes:
The Devil looms large in Shropshire folklore. He appears in many different guises: he is a giant, lumbering over the landscape, moving great masses of land; he is the beast, a terrifying demon, breaking free of his containing circle made by naive and drunken hellraisers; he is God's helper, carrying away the unworthy from the mortal plain. More rarely, he is a suave gentleman, a devious trickster, only to be bested with true repentance and the wisdom of a divine representative. Throughout Shropshire, he leaves his name on the map and stories in his wake .

If you are interested in discovering more about Shropshire myths, legends and folk tales, and where to hear storytelling in Shropshire, the following organisations are a good place to start: Mythstories Museum of Myth and Legend (The Morgan Library, Aston Street, Wem, Shropshire SY4 5AU, Tel. 01939 235500, www.mythstories.com); Festival at the Edge (Tel. 01939 236 626, www.festivalattheedge.org); Society for Storytelling (www.sfs.org.uk).

INDEX